Contents

Warning: This book could seriously improve your life

This book is dedicated to Jo Hardy and to Raffer and Karen. Thank you so much for your support and kindness.

Disclaimer

Only read this book if you are serious about taking powerful and positive steps to leave your fears in the past where they belong, rather than taking them with you into the future.

Challenge of Change

In order to overcome your fear you need to learn to change your behaviour. I challenge you to read this book cover to cover and see how many things you can change while doing so. On every page is a suggestion for a change you can make as you read the words. Challenge yourself to try them, to begin to harness the power of doing things differently.

You can do whatever you want in your own life. Nothing can stop you except for your own fears. Don't blame anyone else ... You have the power to make the decision. Just do it.

Nola Diamontopoulos

Introduction

How often do you find yourself worrying about something you said, or fearing that the past is going to repeat itself, or feeling frightened that you might make a mistake, be disliked or let someone down? Many of us live with fears, and some people are in a state of almost constant fear, anxiety and stress for most of their adult lives. One in ten people has a serious fear or phobia – but many of us also have lesser worries that hold us back and prevent us from performing at our best. You are not alone. Every human being is flawed, every human being has imperfections and insecurities, and fear is a very common problem.

This book is written to help you tackle the fears you don't want. The fears that hold you back, limit you and prevent you from squeezing all the happiness and joy you want from this thing that we call life.

When you are a winner you come back, no matter what happened the day before.

Billy Martin, former baseball player

If your life is ruled by unwelcome fears, you are wasting a lot of your time and energy. Fear, for many of us, is all about trying to deal with the future before it arrives, which is impossible because we can't always predict what lies ahead. You can't control the future by worrying about it. Equally, you can't change the past by dlessly criticizing and judging yourself, and others, for things that happened.

The future is not always a nourishing place to invest your energy. It can be tiring and draining to worry about it. Remember, nothing in life is fixed. Anything can happen, at any time. This can be really exciting if you have lots of confidence in yourself. But if you haven't, the fact you have infinite choices can feel very frightening.

Unfortunately many of us act as if our fears are fixed, as if we are always going to have them. But life is constantly changing. Anything could happen. Everything we do is to some extent a risk or a gamble. However, although you cannot control the world around you, you can learn to control your own fearful reactions, and in the process find serenity, joy and happiness.

One of the best things about the past is that it's over. There is a much better place to focus your attention: the present. It's called the present because the best gift you can give yourself is learning how to be present, in every moment. Rather than being frightened about things that could happen, might happen, or may never happen.

I want to show you that the future is right here, right now. The only thing you have control of is this moment. Not tomorrow, not next week, not next year. Just now.

This very moment is fresh and new, and you actually have the power to do or think whatever you want with it. It's the only moment you need to concern yourself with and you've got as much control over it as you dare to give yourself. I want to encourage you to seize that power by focusing your attention where it can have some effect. Just by picking up this book you're taking your destiny in hand.

I want to show you how to overcome your fears, so that you can be happier and experience more joy and take better care of yourself. This book will show you how to know only possibility and opportunity. To be free from fear – whatever that fear might be.

You might be afraid of failure or rejection, fearful of love or being abandoned, or scared of dying or of the unknown. At times, some of these fears can feel impossible to conquer when you are in the iron grip of the emotion. But there is a way to control and overcome them: To conquer your fear you must first understand it and know how to deal with it when it affects you.

I'm going to explain what fear is, how it starts, and what you can do to change your relationship to it. It may take some time to rewrite the past, but reward yourself with the investment of that time. Be patient. If you plant a seed in the ground you don't expect it to grow immediately. You water it, you nourish it, and give it time to grow.

If you take one thing away from this book I would like it to be an understanding that there is nothing wrong with you. You might think that there is, but really there isn't. What you do is what you think is best.

Without the concentration of the mind and the will, performance would never result.

Roger Bannister, who broke the four-minute mile

So why are people frightened of things? The answer is very simple, it's called practice. You've practised being the way you are so many times that you've become an expert. No one was born with fears or phobias. No one came out of the womb and was frightened of the opposite sex, of failure, of heights or even of death. All of our fears are thoughts and actions we have learned along the way. We may have practised them so well that we have become highly skilful at them.

In fact, some of us probably deserve an Oscar for how effectively we've been doing our fear or fears all these years. But that doesn't mean you want to win an award for it. You're reading this book because you want to change.

What are you prepared to do? Do you actually want to change? Are you prepared to read this book and follow some simple instructions? How much of your focus are you prepared to invest in overcoming your fear? 10 per cent? 20 per cent? 100 per cent? There is only one thing that will stop you investing more: You. The more investment you make in overcoming your fear, the more chance you have of overcoming it, and the quicker you will leave it behind.

What would be the consequences, for you, of getting over your fear? What would changing do for you? What will it give you? Where will it get you? These are some of the questions I want you to answer.

Ultimately people have to want to change, and to understand that they need to be willing and responsible enough to go through the process of change. It often amazes me in my professional work how many people want and expect me to change them. I can't change you, I can't make you read this book, I can't make you do any of the exercises that follow. There are many techniques in this book that can help you, but the techniques on their own won't make any difference. They are just words on a page. It's what you do with the techniques that has the power to make the difference. What you need to do is practise the techniques.

Practice does not make perfect. Practice makes permanent. Perfect practice makes perfect. If you really want to change, you have to practise perfectly – that is, with attention and intention.

You may find some of the things I'm going to explain to you seem very simple and easy. You might think they should be more difficult or complicated.

People often expect things to be complicated. People especially want things to be complicated if they've had their fears for a long time. People with long-term fears have invested a lot into them, and if you've accumulated all this investment it's a very big challenge to let go.

Ask yourself the following question. If you had a pound for every time you've done your fear, how rich would you be? Many of have had our fears for so long and put so much time and energy into them, that they've become a huge investment.

We live in a world where we pride ourselves on our investments – our money, cars, houses – and it can be hard to let go. But in order to become less fearful you need to let go of all the investment you've made in your fear.

Let me ask you this question: what are you going to do instead of being fearful? How would you like to feel?

The only discipline that lasts is self-discipline.

Bum Phillips

If you want to replace your fear with more happiness and joy, for example, read on. But if you are serious about holding on to your fears, and feel that you can't give up all the time and energy you've invested in them, then put the book down, or give it to someone else who is ready to change.

However, I'm confident that if you are really committed to change, that by the time you've used this book you'll be equipped to deal with your life positively, moment by moment.

Reality Check

I want to be straight and up front with you right from the start. It always fascinates me just how many people say that they want to overcome their fear, whether it be of failure, rejection, love, death or any type of fear. But when it actually comes to doing anything about it, how many people just give up, and continue to do what they were doing before?

The easiest thing you can do is to do what you've done before. Anyone can do that. But remember, if you always do what you've always done, you'll always get what you've always got.

The thinking that got you into your fear is not the thinking that's going to get you out of it.

So why do so many people just give up? Believe it or not, many people are scared about losing their fear because they are so used to having it. They have developed a mental comfort blanket around their fears, and the thought of the void that would be left if they were to resolve them successfully can be frightening.

Some people lack the passion and true desire to take control of their lives. Others believe that in order to get rid of their fear they have to face it. They believe that the only way to lose their fears is to experience them. This is simply not the case. I want to help you focus your attention away from your fears, allowing you to change the way you think and act. Ultimately, focusing elsewhere will enable you to become more confident and self-assured.

This book uses quite a lot of stories drawn from the world of sport. It doesn't matter whether you are interested in sport or not, because these stories are actually about learning to manage fear in one of the most fearful arenas of all. Competitive sportspeople understand that achievement in their field is mainly about overcoming, and in some cases using, fear as a tool to bring out their best performance. According to David Lloyd, former top British tennis player: 'It's better to have a strong mind than natural talent. 80 per cent of the game is in the mind.'

My Story

Our internal fears often start at a very young age.

My father always used to say to visitors about me, 'he's yours for half a crown.' He was only joking – wasn't he? The more you hear something – even as a joke – the more it undermines your confidence.

There is too much emphasis on success and failure, and too little on how a person grows as he works. Enjoy the journey, enjoy every moment and quit worrying.

Matt Biondi, Olympic gold medallist

I always felt different. But eventually I realized I *am* different. I'm a human being and we're all flawed because of the nature of how we learn. It took me a long time to discover this.

I was born four weeks early by emergency Caesarean. They couldn't find my heartbeat, and for two days while I was in intensive care my mother didn't see me. I was swept off into an incubator before I could be held in her arms, or hear the reassurance of her heartbeat. She was so worried that something was wrong with her little baby.

Before you were born you were safe in the womb. All of a sudden you are thrust into this cold world, desperate to be cocooned again.

My first memories are of being very frustrated. *I want to explore but I'm stuck miles above the ground in a high-chair. My mother drops something on the floor and winces. She seems unhappy. I start to cry. She is the centre of my world. My reactions are connected to hers. I can sense that she is worried about me when I play or explore. She is worried because she loves me. I don't appreciate the subtlety of this and just think the world is full of danger.*

When I was four, I recall struggling in nursery school. *I am bored and impatient. I have so much energy and I don't know what to do with it. There must be something wrong with me.*

When I was six my teachers seemed very unhappy with me. They are there to make you conform, think and act in a certain way, but their rules made no sense to me. *I don't understand what they are talking about. I'm not interested in what I am supposed to be doing. I speak out because I am confused and unhappy, and want to communicate my boredom. I get into trouble. I am too scared to tell them how I feel anymore.*

Soon I was just scared of teachers, full stop. I wasn't doing anything right, so they sent me down a year and told my mother I had learning difficulties. The educational psychologist said I had poor attention to detail. He didn't believe in dyslexia.

I picked up that there was something wrong with me.

This was frightening. I suppressed the feeling because it made me feel uneasy. How was I to know that this was going to affect my life for years? It didn't make me feel good, why would I want to think about it?

I was sent to a new school. *My handwriting is so bad that I have to have extra lessons outside school. I am so frustrated. Everyone seems so disappointed in me, and worried. I can't spell. I can't read. I can't do any of the things that people seem to think I should be able to do.*

When I was 10, I was diagnosed as having dyslexia by an educational psychologist. I didn't know what it meant to have a high IQ, all I knew was that I found reading and spelling difficult. I was being conditioned to value academic attainment, something that I couldn't deliver. But I wasn't allowed to express myself my own way. *I have to go out of school to have a special lesson that no one else is having. I realize something really is wrong with me. I do badly in my exams. Apparently I need to concentrate more, but I don't know how. My mother is trying to protect me from things at which I might fail. She seems fearful for me. Now I'm really worried.*

Because I was frightened and miserable I responded by becoming very naughty, seeking a different form of attention. It was becoming clear that I was exceptionally gifted at two things: mucking about and being fearful, and I used one to mask the other.

When I was 11 a different educational psychologist suggested I go to a less academic school. I was sent to a comprehensive a year after the other boys in my year. *I'm being bullied. Trying to fit in when you already feel such a misfit is difficult. I've got a big nose and I'm Jewish. They call me names. I don't fight back because the bullies are right: There is something wrong with me.*

We must either find a way or make one.

Hannibal

I desperately wanted people to like me, so I started laughing at myself. *Wanting people to like me becomes more important because I've got a secret: I've noticed that one of my testicles is getting bigger than the other. I feel deeply ashamed, and worried.*

The testicle increases in size over the next five years. I tell no one. Fear over what this might mean rumbles away inside me all the time, but in a way that's OK: I already knew there was something wrong with me and this merely reinforces that feeling.

I got in with the wrong crowd, seeking to belong through destructive behaviours such as smoking and drinking, pretending to be macho and hard. Like so many thousands of insecure boys, I'd found something I could do and be good at. Fortunately, there was always something in me that stopped me pushing the extremes. I wanted the badge of belonging, nothing more. I also discovered I had a ready wit. I had started wearing masks, although I couldn't see it at the time. For years I wasn't myself, because I thought there was something wrong with who I really was. I coped by covering up my weakness and pretending to be something that I wasn't. *I don't like what's going on inside my head. This means I want to get out of my head.* Drugs, food and alcohol seemed to help.

The self-fulfilling prophecy of O-levels came true: I got none, as predicted. I was merely fulfilling people's expectations. I was shunted into taking a school certificate offered to people with learning difficulties. It was ugly, and suddenly for the first time I saw a future. I realized that I could achieve more than this. I managed to talk my way onto a college course in sports and recreational studies.

I was not the brightest student, but I had so much energy. For the first time in my life I was determined to achieve something. Two years later I took a vocational course equivalent to A-levels. During this time I also plucked up courage to go to a doctor.

I was 17 years old and I was petrified. The doctor took one look at my enlarged testicle and said, 'I think this is very serious, I think you may have cancer.' I phoned my mother and told her I was dying. Her fear entwined with my own for the next 24 hours. But relief came when I returned to the doctor. The cyst was benign.

I should have felt relieved, but I was so used to feeling different and weird and frightened that I didn't know how to stop the feelings. I was so good at my fear that I couldn't give it up that easily. My fear had become a habit. We develop fears and anxieties through practice and repetition.

Meanwhile, I was discovering some measure of success academically for the first time. It was bloody hard work, but I thought I'd be OK if I could pass exams like anyone else. It was to take me another 10 years to realize that I wasn't living a life true to myself, but one ruled by the fear of external expectations.

I started a diploma in higher education. I really struggled with my essays and assignments, but I was determined to prove everyone else wrong.

At the age of 20 I started a sports science degree. I'd been working as a fitness and aerobics instructor in a health club and forging my own destiny with infectious enthusiasm. After graduating I was working an 80-hour week as a fitness instructor. I couldn't afford to stop for a moment.

On the inside I was still terrified. I had become a people pleaser. I'd always found it easy to get on with people because I wanted them, more than anything, to like me. *I go out of my way to show them how nice I am. I am so frightened they will reject me. If they don't like me their attitude will reaffirm my life-long fear that there is something wrong with me.*

The crisis of yesterday is the joke of tomorrow.

H.G. Wells

The fear was with me every moment of every day. Outwardly I looked confident, but I was bubbling over on the inside, constantly trying to stop the pot from boiling over. Inevitably, I started to get ill. I began a teaching degree because I wanted to go back into schools to try and help kids like me. But I wasn't listening to what was really going on within myself. I was trying to please the world, focused on seeking recognition through achievement. I was seeking external endorsement that I was OK, because my life had taught me that it wasn't OK to be me. I know now that this is very common behaviour – but I had no clue then.

At the age of 24, I started to get some serious health problems. I'd developed a habit of trying to sort out everyone's problems but my own. I felt responsible for people. My mother is Jewish – she's responsible for everybody – and I'd discovered I too had empathic gifts. I started helping people lose weight, and this opened up a counselling role. I was teaching psychology to other people. I was always on the move, with lots of clients dependent on me. *For all my knowledge, it is still easier for me to focus my attention outwards on my clients, than to face my fear that I'm not good enough.*

I ended up with chronic fatigue syndrome. I was saved by not being able to get out of bed. In those dark moments, I started to look at the world in a completely different way. I had no clients to focus on. I couldn't escape myself. I began to examine my thought processes. I realized that I'd invested a lot of time in feeling fearful. I'd developed a comfort zone around it. It became clear that the only way to change my life was to detach myself from my fear. I realized that I needed to completely reassess many of the lessons I had absorbed when I was small, and attempt to reorganize my thinking.

For the first time in my life I accepted that in order to live a life without fear I would have to admit the truth to myself, and commit myself to change.

My story is not remotely unusual. It could be the story of a thousand people, just like me. I wasn't physically attacked or abused, but I had learned how to be scared nonetheless.

I thought I was weird. I thought I was different. I thought everyone else was confident and had it together, and that I was a failure. I now know it's OK to be me. But for so long I had no idea about this. You might be experiencing some of the feelings I used to have, but you can change the way you feel just as I did. I've experienced fear from the inside out. I've been there, too.

Today I believe I am living proof that by taking your life into your own hands and learning how to take care of yourself you can have more joy, happiness and spontaneity than you ever could have imagined.

In the course of the book I will give you a deeper understanding of what fear is, where it comes from, how you can control it and how you can learn to use it to your advantage.

Throughout the book I am going to introduce you to techniques and exercises that will help you run your life more effectively.

You currently run your life the way you do because you believe it's best. You live like this because your brain believes that this is the most effective strategy for you. But you don't *have* to be fearful; you've just *learned* to be. It is possible to be happy and function effectively, and to not be ruled by fear.

To gain real benefit from this book, it's important to follow through to the end. Be positive. If you get stuck or don't understand something, don't give up. The chances are that you've put a lot of effort and time into developing your fears; it's only reasonable that you should give yourself some time to change.

However, by following the steps in the book, and finding the exercises that work best for you, you really do have the opportunity to build your self-confidence, become more optimistic and strengthen your personal conviction. By understanding what fear really is, you can learn to use it to your advantage and ultimately nourish your life.

At this point, let me congratulate you that you are giving yourself an opportunity to change. Perhaps it's a second chance, or perhaps third, fourth or even fortieth chance to make your life the way you want it to be. Some people never give themselves that opportunity, and continue to live a life unfulfilled or under the shadow of fear.

You are the person who is going to make the difference. This book cannot change your life; **you** will change your life, and this book will help you. You've learned the fear, you've practised it: You can change it.

The will to win is important, but the will to prepare to win is vital.

Joe Paterno

Why Fear Is Frightening

He who will not apply new remedies must expect new evils.

Francis Bacon

You were born into the world fearless. All that you knew was unlimited possibility. You could become anyone, go anywhere, or do anything. You didn't *know* that you could, but equally you didn't know that you *couldn't*. You didn't know the difference between good and bad, right and wrong, positive or negative. You didn't understand trust, guilt or values. Education meant nothing to you.

Instead, you just did exactly what you wanted to do, when you wanted to do it, on your own terms. You slept. You cried because you were hungry or because you needed to be held or because you needed your nappy changing. When offered milk you'd drink only if you felt like it. You were in control of your own universe. You thought you *were* the universe.

But gradually, you began to learn that your world consisted not just of yourself, but of objects and other people. Your mother became very important in your life, because she provided you with food, warmth and love that were profoundly nourishing.

But as you grew, along with this new awareness came something else. Rules arrived. They stated 'This is not the way' and you made a discovery: that you were not OK how you were. Your parents wanted to mould you, to prepare you in the best way they thought possible for the world. They thought it would be easier for you if you were like other people. They insisted that they wanted you to be like them. You had to eat when they wanted to eat, what they wanted you to eat. Maybe it's true to say that you resented this; for a time you certainly fought against it, but as demands were continually placed on you, you learned how to be obedient, to comply or conform to a way that was alien to you at the time, but became second nature to you with practice.

When you were a baby aged between newborn and three, you didn't have problems or fears. Things were just the way they were. The way you learned was by imitating the people and the world around you.

But by the time you started school, you had already been exposed to attitudes, values and modes of expected behaviour that had been programmed into you, influencing the way you thought and acted. As you grew older you absorbed most of your beliefs second-hand. Family, rules, culture, religion, values and education all told you how to act and react. You learned to distrust your own senses and, in many cases, became frightened of being yourself. Instead of trusting your native wits, you were being encouraged to rely on second-hand information.

You had no say in so much of what you experienced, you didn't know ultimately if it would serve you or not.

Chances are you moved into adult life believing that deep down you were flawed in some way. And if you have the notion you are not good enough, you are going to be frightened.

Fear Comes in Many Forms

A mission could be defined as an image of a desired state that you want to get to. Once fully seen it will inspire you to act, fuel your motivation and determine your behaviour.

Charles Garfield

Fear can come as a shiver in the delight of anticipation, or as the complete opposite, as all-consuming terror. It can feel like butterflies in the pit of your stomach, or like full-scale churning anxiety. At its extreme it is delivered up as a panic attack, with horrifying palpitations. Fear can present itself as shame when you realize you have failed and feel alone. Or it can loom darkly, threatening punishment, as guilt. It can come suddenly – as it does when your life is in danger – or it can gnaw away at you, with little apparent cause and even less resolution.

But for most of us, fear is a nervousness that underscores much of what we do. People say they feel 'anxious' or 'stressed'. What they are really telling us is that they feel frightened. We have these fears because we are adult human beings.

And although education, culture, religion and family values give us plenty of insights, they can't always help us deal effectively with the complexity of life, or leave us able to give ourselves the support that we need. However, given that our bodies and brains haven't evolved at the same rate as our social environment, it's amazing that we are not more frightened.

What is the biggest fear in the Western world? Surprisingly, it's not a fear of dying a painful death or losing a loved one. For the majority of people, the fear that unites more of us than anything else is the fear of exposing ourselves so that people can see our flaws and fears. Perhaps this is why so many people are frightened of public speaking. The fear of speaking out is a fear of believing we are not good enough.

You might think there is something wrong with you, but there is something wrong with all of us. We are frightened of ourselves. But there is no need to be frightened.

My experience of working with many top athletes and sporting champions is that many of them are frightened to admit they've got a problem or a weakness. As we grow up we are taught to hide our fears, insecurities and imperfections. It's the 'pull your socks up', 'stiff upper lip' mentality. But however much you try to hide it, the fear remains. For athletes, it surfaces in the heat of competition when they are under stress.

Women tend to be much better about admitting their fears, partly because we live in a culture where men in general do find it pretty difficult to admit to having a problem or needing help. But women also face a challenge, brought up in a culture that prizes strict ideas of feminine beauty so highly. They conform to wearing certain clothes and trying to live within cultural expectations. This can lead them to feel inadequate, which is the fear of believing they are not good enough just the way they are. Men don't escape, however, because the cultural pressure on them is to succeed. They don't feel good enough either, because in our culture they are conditioned to ignore fear and to turn it into anger. They are supposed to be strong, protective and aggressive. They are trained to take fearful emotions and channel them into aggression on the sports field or in traffic. Mostly it's a waste of energy.

A friend was telling me about the child of a friend of his. The boy was about nine or ten, and had been watching and observing the life that his parents led. The mother was constantly going from one diet to another, not happy with her appearance, and seemed to be constantly giving herself a hard time. The father worked ridiculously long hours, and was under constant stress and anxiety. At times he would lash out in frustration. The parents would argue in front of their son. On one occasion the father saw the boy was upset and told him he needed to grow up. The child turned to both parents and said: 'I don't want to grow up and be part of your world. What's so good about it? You're unhappy. I need a hug. I need love, I need fun. I want to feel happy. That's the world I want to live in.'

You'll only become a winner if you're willing to walk over the edge.

Damon Runyon

Most children lose this innate wisdom and perspective as they grow up. They learn that showing fear or being frightened is a weakness. This means that fear, like death, is for many people a great unmentionable. So you invent a whole raft of excuses for not facing up to the fact that you are frightened. You might get ill, develop allergies, or come up with apparently logical reasons for following one course of behaviour or totally steering clear of the thing that frightens you, all to hide the fact that deep down you are scared.

Choices

Today is the tomorrow that you were so scared of yesterday.

David Mead

You didn't have much of a choice as to the environment in which you were raised. But now you *do* have a choice. You can re-invent yourself. You can be anything you want to be.

If someone stepped heavily on your toe you would cry 'Ouch!' When we feel pain inside, though, sometimes we won't do that. We keep it inside, rather than let it out.

I spent most of my life frightened that there was something wrong with me. I was so afraid that I was unable to tell anyone of my fear. Because I lived with my fear for such a long time, the high levels of adrenaline – a natural internal stimulant – in my system added more stress until eventually I realized I was physically and mentally exhausted. This is an effect called Boiled Frog syndrome. If you put a frog in a pot of hot water it will jump out. But if you put the same frog in a bowl of cold water and gradually increase the temperature, the frog's blood temperature will increase at the same rate without the frog realizing or even feeling uncomfortable. Eventually the water is so hot that the frog is cooked. His system is so proficient at adapting to the conditions in which he finds himself that it actually proves his downfall. When human beings are constantly exposed to stressful situations they also learn to adapt – just watch the mother of a toddler who copes with high levels of noise and chaos while carrying on normal conversations with her friends. For the human being, the long-term effects of stress silently accumulate (just like the water increasing in temperature in the pot) until one day you realize you are living your life in fear.

You're cooked. But unlike the frog, who doesn't realize until it's too late to do anything about his situation, the challenge for us is to realize that we do not have to feel like this.

What precedes all behaviours, actions and performances? What turns a dream into a reality? The answer is *choices*. The choices you make determine what you think, how you feel, what you do and whom you become. Whether it is something you say to yourself, something you picture or something you feel before you find yourself doing it, you have control – a lot more control than you may be aware of.

Whether we admit it or not, we all select our jobs, our relationships and our living environments. We are also responsible for how we react to them. If our lives are full of stress and anxiety (or adrenaline), we alone put it there. It is our own adrenaline that creates our own turmoil.

Stress, anxiety and fear are not, for the most part, a result of uncontrollable external forces. It is not 'them' or 'it' or 'they' who produce our stressful reactions. It is us.

Taking Control

The greatest professional quality is not money but attitude.

John Monie

I urge you to leave the shackles of your bad experiences behind you. One of the best things about the past is that it is in the past. It's time to take control.

Taking control of something is all about recognizing its

symptoms and becoming aware of its presence. When you understand it, you can begin to change your relationship to it.

But sometimes the noise in our heads is so great – all the chattering, bullying and self-criticism that's going on internally – that we haven't got the space even to begin to change.

I'm going to introduce you to a number of exercises as the book progresses. You might find some of them are useful for you, and others are not. Be patient. If you struggle with one, just move on.

I'd like you to try something now. In the West, many of us spend a lot of time thinking. Most of our attention is in our head. But this something you did not do as a small child. Back then, you lived moment by moment, acting instinctively and breathing deeply and naturally. You just observed the world you lived in. You were fully present and in touch with all of your senses. The Chinese have always been well known for being very observant in this way. But in our culture, we are taught how to be critical and analytical.

In the next exercise I want to show you what happens when you move your focus away from your head, and into the centre of your body.

Finding Your Centre

Now, as silly and strange as this might sound, I'd like you to find a marker pen. Stand up and place your hand across your navel. Pull up your shirt and make two tiny marks, one that is roughly 2 inches below and the other 4 inches above your belly button.

Now sit down. I want you to focus on breathing in between the two lines. Imagine the air is water pouring down into your belly, which expands like a bag filling up with liquid. That's all I want you to do. Direct your focus of attention between those two marks on your tummy as you breathe in and out, slowly and gently.

Notice what happens when you start doing that. Your mind instantly quietens down and you can sense it feels good and you are relaxed.

The way this exercise encourages you to breathe is the natural way to breathe. It's the way you were born to breathe. It's only through experiencing stress and anxiety in the world that we've learned to breathe in a shallow way, in our chests. Often when you are worried about the way you look, you suck in your tummy. This actually makes it impossible to breathe properly.

Athletes who achieve one point of attention are able to be completely present. This state has been called 'flow' or 'being in the zone', but champions call this place home.

Breathing into this part of your body, namely around your navel, is what the Chinese call the tan t'ien, which is the centre or the middle of the body. This is where the Chinese believe the source of your energy flows from. I was speaking at a workshop recently and there was a Chinese woman at the front of the audience who was very spontaneous and happy. She explained that in her culture you just know that this is where you're strong, and she pointed to her midriff.

Moving your focus of attention away from your mind and into your body also encourages you to listen more to your senses. Your senses don't tell lies. It's your mind that misleads you. It can create fantasies and illusions, some of which are not at all helpful.

Throughout the book, and for the rest of your life, I strongly recommend that you practise breathing into this part of your body.

When you see Sumo wrestlers slapping their torso, or Chinese martial artists breaking something, they are always moving their focus down into the centre of their body, the tan t'ien. They believe this central panel is the source of their energy and strength. Tai Chi movement comes from here, so does Kung Fu and Karate.

The Power of Your Senses

Thinking too much can stop us from enjoying our life. Talking to ourselves and constantly analysing can cloud our senses. It is estimated that children use a greater percentage of their senses, about 25 per cent, but by the time we are adults we use just 12.5 per cent. Why? Because adults tend to think too much. The truth is that it is very difficult to think and use our senses effectively at the same time. What was Archimedes doing when he had his scientific revelation? He wasn't hunched over his desk with an inky quill in his hand. He was dozing in the bath. Similarly, what was Einstein doing when the theory of relativity came to him? He was day-dreaming that he was riding on a beam of light.

For both these men, it was relaxing and visualizing that let the critical, analytical part of their minds switch off. This allowed their inspiration and creativity to flow freely.

Our ability to relax affects our willingness to trust.

Analysing is examining something in detail.

Anal-ising is going over and over something in the absence of any new information.

I want to encourage you to be more observant, in using your power of awareness so you start to sense what frightens you and how you become frightened of it. Ultimately, I want to help you give yourself some space so you can think and act in a different way.

Taking Control of Fear

I want you to become an imaginary secret agent. Your mission, should you choose to accept it, is to observe how you 'do' your fear and ultimately become frightened. You don't have to avoid the feelings, but rather learn how to observe them. When you start feeling nervous and anxious, don't focus on trying to avoid these unpleasant feelings. Instead, make a mental note about how you are feeling. Try and isolate the different physical and emotional experiences that are occurring. Perhaps you feel a tightening in your stomach, maybe your mind starts to race a bit, or you get the urge to distract yourself.

If it's helpful to you, record the key sensations here

_____

_____

Remember, you are not trying to stop the feelings, and you are not criticizing yourself for having them. You are simply recording your responses. By acknowledging fear and keeping good company with it, you might begin to see ways in which you can control it.

We are brought up in a society where you have to stay strong and put on a brave face, however you feel on the inside. You might be feeling you are working hard not to let the pot bubble over, as I did, or to stop yourself shattering into a thousand tiny pieces. You are not alone. The difference between you and anyone else, is that you are ready to admit that there's a problem: that your life can be ruled by fear.

The Temple of the Golden Buddha

In 1957, a group of monks in Thailand had to relocate a large clay Buddha from their temple to a new location, as their monastery was being replaced by a highway to Bangkok. It began to rain. The head monk decided to cover the sacred Buddha with a large canvas to protect it. Later that evening he went to check on it, shining his torch under the canvas to see if the Buddha was still dry. He noticed a gleam catch the light and wondered whether there might be something under the clay. Using a chisel and hammer he started to chip it away. As he knocked off shards of clay, the gleam grew brighter and brighter. Hours later, the monk was standing face to face with an extraordinary solid gold Buddha that measured 10 feet tall and weighed over two-and-a-half tonnes.

Experts believe that, several hundred years earlier when the Burmese army was about to invade Thailand, the monks of the time had covered their precious golden Buddha with a coating of clay to protect it. The secret remained intact until 1957.

We are all like the clay Buddha, covered with a protective shell of hardness created out of fear. Yet inside each of us is a golden Buddha, which is our real self. Somewhere along the way, between the ages of two and nine, we begin to cover up the golden essence of our natural selves. Just like the monk with the hammer and chisel, your goal is to find your true essence once again.

As long as I can focus on enjoying what I'm doing, having fun, I know I'll play well.

Steffi Graf

What Do You Really Want?

All pressure is self-inflicted. It's what you make of it or how you let it run off on you.

Sebastian Coe

Imagine feeling free, instead of afraid. Imagine feeling excited about your life. Imagine seeing the unknown as an opportunity to grow and develop, rather than something to be frightened about. Taking time to understand your fear is the first step to moving to a place not only free from it, but where you can rediscover a different way of living.

Looking honestly at what your fear is giving you and where it came from is the first important step towards spring-cleaning and updating your approach to your fearful feelings. Fear is something we practise so often that it's usually become something of a habit. Once you can see it in that diminished context, it becomes easier to think about beginning to break your dependency on it.

Become aware of your breathing for a moment. Are you breathing deeply, as I suggested earlier, or are your breaths shallow once again? Most of us breathe from our chest, and although breathing that way is probably OK, it's not as nourishing as breathing deep into your stomach and expanding your lungs to their full capacity.

We breathe the way we do through habit, not because it is necessarily the best way. Because of the way our brains work, we tend to make the choices we've made before. When you behave in a certain way for the first time, you form a connection to that way of thinking. You do it again, then again, and again and again. And it becomes second nature.

My dog died in 1987, but even 13 years later whenever I went to my parents' house I still expected the dog to be there. I would laugh at myself when this happened, and feel rather stupid. Perhaps we should face the fact that we are all sometimes a little silly and stupid, every single one of us. Many of us behave in ways that have nothing to do with common sense.

What I'd like you to try and do is see your fearful behaviour as nothing more than a habit. This is a real challenge if you've lived with a fear for a long time, because we tend to take it seriously and think there is something wrong with us.

During the 1970s, a number of fishing boats were shot at as they passed by a Pacific island long thought uninhabited. The shootings were reported and the Japanese military realized what had happened. During the Second World War, a number of Japanese troops had been sent to occupy and guard little islands in the Pacific. They had been instructed to shoot at invaders or enemies of Japan. Some of these garrisons were still in existence, but they didn't realize that the war had ended decades earlier. Instead of rushing in to instruct the soldiers to stop fighting, a former sergeant donned an old uniform and travelled to the island to thank the men for their actions. He then explained that the war was over. Their conditioned behaviour could then be replaced by actions and experiences more in keeping with the outside world.

Often we act in ways that are no longer useful to us, continuing because we have no way of knowing we have a choice about how we behave.

If you can see your fear as something you have practised, and maybe even raise a smile about how long you've been practising this self-defeating behaviour, then just like the soldiers in the story you will have gained the power to begin to change. Oh yes, and practise breathing more deeply!

It's Up to You

Never let yesterday use up too much of today.

Will Rogers

No one else can make your fear vanish. The commitment can only come from you. But taking responsibility doesn't have to be a difficult process. Just beginning to look objectively at your fear can help you cut it right down to size.

The 20 Most Important Questions about Fear

Take a few moments to consider the following questions. Jot down your reactions to each question in the space provided (use the blank pages at the back of the book if you need more space). There are no right or wrong answers. Everything you need to know about your fear is inside you. The more honest you can be with yourself, the more you will be helping yourself.

1. What is the fear that you want to get rid of?
2. Do you believe you were born with this fear? Yes/No
3. Have you learned this fear? Yes/No
4. How have you practised this fear? Yes/No
5. Are you good at this fear? Yes/No. Mark on the following one to ten scale (1 being not very, 10 being all-consuming) how intense this fear is for you.
    1 2 3 4 5 6 7 8 9 10
6. How does this fear nourish you?

7. What impact does this fear have on your life? Physically?
    Emotionally? Practically?
8. How will this fear serve your needs in the future?
9. Do you want to conquer your fear? Yes / No
10. Are you willing to conquer your fear? Yes / No
11. Why have you chosen now to help yourself?
12. Are you prepared to change? Yes / No
13. Do you expect to conquer your fear?
14. Are you prepared to do whatever it takes?
15. What would be different in your life as a result of
    overcoming your fear?
16. What would it do for you, what would it give you, what
    would it get you?
17. In order to gain those benefits, are you prepared to let go
    of your fears and put your focus of attention somewhere
    else?
18. On a scale of one to ten (one being not very, ten being
    completely) how motivated are you to change?
    1 2 3 4 5 6 7 8 9 10
19. On a scale of one to ten how ready are you to change?
    1 2 3 4 5 6 7 8 9 10
20. How will you know when your fear has been resolved?

Considering these questions is a great way to re-focus on what
your fears really are: Behaviours and habits you have practised
to the point that they feel like a fundamental part of you.

Why Fear Is Normal

Fear is normal. Everyone has the capacity to feel frightened, as a reaction, fear is a natural protection mechanism that we were born with, we inherited it from our ancestors who needed it for their survival. But the fear reaction, and our specific fears, can become habits that hold us back. When you do something over and over again it becomes deeply engrained into your behaviour. When that happens it can be difficult to know what you would do without it. This is called the comfort zone. You've put so much investment into your fear that if the fear was money you'd be very rich. As I said before, you are not wrong for doing this. It's just what you have been doing – up until now.

If you want, today can be the first day of the rest of your life.

It doesn't matter how long you have had the fear. The key to recovery is being prepared to change. The majority of people who say they want to change, don't. This is how strong a habit fear is, and though it's hard to break a habit this engrained, I know you can keep going and can work through it.

Releasing Your Fear

I would like you to imagine that you can drain fear out of your body.

1. Sit comfortably with both feet on the floor.
2. Focus on your breathing, breathing into your stomach, filling it up with air, as if it were a bag of water.
3. When you feel relaxed and comfortable, recall something you are frightened of. What colour would you associate the fear with? Would you say it is green, black, red, orange or some other colour? If a colour doesn't come to mind, that's fine. Just focus on breathing deeply. As you're breathing out, imagine you've got holes in your feet and imagine all of the fear is being drained out of your body and into the earth.
4. As you breathe out just say to yourself, inside your head, the words 'relax' or 'calm'. Imagine sending the soothing ripples of this word all the way down to your toes, and up to your nose and into your hands.

Our Deepest Fear

Our deepest fear is not that we are inadequate. Our deepest fear is that we are powerful beyond measure. It is our light, not our darkness, that most frightens us. We ask ourselves, who am I to be brilliant, gorgeous, talented, fabulous? Actually, who are you not to be? You are a child of God. Your playing small doesn't serve the world. There's nothing enlightened about shrinking so that other people won't feel insecure around you. We are all meant to shine, as children do. We were born to make manifest the glory of God that is within us. It's not just in some of us; it's in everyone. And as we let our own light shine, we unconsciously give other people permission to do the same. As we're liberated from our own fear, our presence automatically liberates others.

Nelson Mandela, 1994 Inaugural speech

2

How Do You 'Do' Your Fear?

When I dare to be powerful, to use my strength in the service of my vision, then it becomes less and less important whether I am afraid.

Audre Lorde

As we have discovered, most fears develop when we are very young, formed either from experiences that happen to us, or attitudes that we absorb second-hand from other people. From a young age we are taught a value system that comes from education, religion, culture and other people. This is not to say that it's all good or bad, or right or wrong. It means that from very early on we start trying to be something we are not. We begin to conform, to try to fit in. But fitting in seems to be a real struggle, because it's unnatural and takes us away from our true self. No one can be like anyone else, because everyone is different.

Recently, I was watching some seven-year-olds on the other side of the canal where I used to live. They were screaming, jumping up and down, and freely expressing themselves. I observed their mother shouting at them to sit and be quiet. Whenever they started to make a noise, she started telling them off again. Our culture demands that we have to learn to be seen and not heard, to be quiet when we are told to be quiet, and to learn to get things right, not wrong. To conform, to fit in. Many of us have been encouraged to think and act like adults, to live our lives like a game of Simon says, not to openly express ourselves and be creative. How many adults do you know who like and appreciate themselves, and are fearless? Chances are, not very many. Compare this to very young children. You probably find many more of them are happy. They are not struggling to conform, they are just being themselves and they don't worry what anybody thinks.

Because conformity feels so difficult – it *is* difficult! The struggle to fit in makes many people think there is something wrong with them.

A natural reaction to this is to feel frightened.

Recently I watched a children's television programme about scorpions. Well, I can tell you, it would have made anyone frightened. There was scary music, a sinister voice-over, lots of startling close-up shots. Although we can become frightened of things that have actually hurt us, we can also become frightened of things if we are *taught* they are scary. Even if they actually present minimal risk to us, our brains can't draw a distinction. Because spiders, like the scorpions in that programme, are universally depicted as something to be scared of, from a very early age many people are frightened of them despite the fact that they've never had a genuinely fearful encounter with one. We can learn our fearful attitudes second hand.

Many fears are less tangible things than spiders or heights, but they are laid down in our minds in a similar way. We learn all sorts of things as we grow up, about science, history, maths, etc. But we are given very little training in stuff that helps us deal with life. We're not taught about how to create great relationships, or strategies on how to deal with failure or success, or about coping with an unknown future. Also we are not taught how to enjoy our lives.

Life Lessons

Imaginary obstacles are insurmountable. Real ones aren't. But you can't tell the difference when you have no real information. Fear can create even more imaginary obstacles than ignorance can. That's why the smallest step away from speculation and into reality can be an amazing relief.

Barbara Sher

We learn lessons according to how life treats us. If bad things happen to us, we learn to avoid situations that might make us feel like that again.

If you're a baby and you burn your hand, you won't put it near a fire again. If you're a child and your parents get divorced, it's profoundly traumatic and you'll do anything to avoid experiencing those feelings again. The same bit of your brain that protects you from real, physical dangers also protects you from things you've learned are emotionally uncomfortable.

We develop fears because we think they will protect us from being hurt, or perhaps even from death.

But these reactions are not always appropriate and beneficial. If you fail at something, do you really believe that you should avoid all situations that might lead to failure in the future? In order to get things right you are going to have to make mistakes first. It's like learning an instrument, learning to walk or learning to bake a cake. To begin with, almost everything you do will be wrong, but it is only by making these mistakes that you begin to refine your technique.

You are a product of everything that you have experienced. What have you experienced? Rules, ideas, values, culture, education, religion. If you could live your life again from the beginning, would you change things? What would you do differently?

Letting Yourself Be Less Than Perfect

The worst thing that can happen to you as an enthusiastic adult is that you could appear foolish to people who need to criticize. Let me assure you – enthusiasm is worth this risk. If you allow yourself to be enthusiastic, you'll be so full of wonder, you won't care what people think.

Barbara Sher

Unfortunately, our culture programmes us to give ourselves a hard time if we make a mistake. Deep down, many of us believe that making a mistake means admitting that there is something wrong with us. We're actually desperately frightened of admitting that there is something wrong with us because we fear it will mark us out as different. But the fact is that there is something 'wrong' with us all.

We often think the way we are is the way we are supposed to be. But in fact, your personality is shaped in response to the way you've chosen to filter your experiences in life. You can't change what's happened in your life, but you can change your relationship to those events. More importantly, you can change the relationship you have with yourself.

Recently I worked with David, a client in his fifties. He asked me, 'Would it be more difficult for you to motivate somebody of my age?'

I explained that it doesn't matter what age someone is. What matters is whether they are *prepared* to change. In fact, someone who is older is likely to have an even clearer desire to make changes in their life, as they have probably experienced their fears so many times that they are more inclined to change their self-defeating ways. They have more evidence that it is an unproductive way to live.

Did you hear about the man who prayed to the goddess asking to win the lottery? OK, said the goddess. When he didn't win he prayed again, begging for success the next week. Yes, all right, said the goddess. Another week passed, and still the man had not won. He asked the goddess why. 'For goodness sake,' she said. 'Meet me halfway. Buy a ticket!' You may think this book is your winning ticket, but the real winning ticket is whether you are willing and ready to take responsibility.

Many people think that someone is going to fix them, or going to buy them the winning ticket. They find it difficult to take responsibility for change. It is easier in many cases to carry on doing what you've been doing, or to blame others or to blame circumstances, than it is to be willing to make changes. As we've already mentioned, you are the way you are because you've practised being like that. But these values and ways of behaving do not define who you are. You are so much more than the sum of all your experiences.

I often come across people who think they know everything, and always have to be right. But no one knows everything. Science can only explain an estimated 5 per cent of how the mind and body actually work. What does this mean? It means we have no idea of the scale of the limitless potential that lies within us all.

What can you do? You can start to make the whole process just that bit easier for yourself by imagining getting over your fear, not as a problem, but as a challenge. The simple truth is: if you carry on doing what you have always done, you are likely to continue to get the same results. What will make things different is learning how to behave differently.

When they are young, elephants being trained for life in a circus are attached to a stake in the ground by a heavy chain. As much as they try to pull away they cannot, until one day they give up trying. From then on they can be chained up with nothing more than a rope; whenever the elephant thereafter experiences any degree of resistance, it gives up trying to fight it, even though it has the strength to pull the entire circus tent over. These elephants are *conditioned* to believe it is impossible to pull away, and their behaviour follows the belief. They stop trying because they don't believe they can succeed.

Success, in my view, is the willingness to strive for something you really want. The person not reaching the top is no less a success than the one who came first – if they both sweated

blood, sweat and tears, and overcame obstacles and fears. Failure to be perfect does not mean you're not a success.

Fran Tarkenton

'You'll never amount to anything'; 'You can't sing'; 'You're not clever enough'; 'You should have more realistic goals'; 'You're the reason our marriage broke up'; 'If I hadn't had children I'd have had a chance.' These 'scripts' are being read aloud all over Britain. The stakes are being driven into the ground, the heavy chains firmly attached, until we reach the point where we believe we cannot pull free.

You need to change your perspective, and grasp the striking fact that all that holds you back is the merest thread. The chain is an illusion, and can easily be broken if you choose to break it.

Are you ready to choose to change?

The Fear of Change

What do you think is the biggest hurdle between you and conquering your fear? What do you think most people in general are frightened of? Most people are frightened of change. You may find the idea of change uncomfortable, even if it means getting rid of the pain and discomfort that your fear causes you.

There is a very simple explanation for why people don't overcome their fears. It's because we are very much creatures of comfort. We formulate ways of thinking and acting which become habits. Our brains often go to great lengths to try and protect us, even when we'd be better off doing something else.

You may feel like dwelling on your limits or your fears. Don't do it ... A perfect prescription for a squandered, unfulfilled life is to accommodate self-defeating feelings while undercutting your finest, most productive ones.

Marsha Sinetar

Does staying within your inherited or learned comfort zones stop you from conquering your fear? This next exercise shows how we instinctively regard change as threatening, and how the brain searches always for what is familiar and comfortable.

Thumbs

1. Interlock your fingers, with one thumb sitting on top of the other.
2. Notice how that feels. It should feel normal, comfortable and nice.
3. Now, unlock your hands and put them back together so that the other thumb is on top. How does that feel?
4. Chances are that it feels distinctly uncomfortable, as though the thumb and two forefingers are in the wrong place.
5. Now go back to the other way. This feels better, when all the fingers are in the right place.

This exercise has been done by thousands of people and nearly everyone, without me even suggesting it, goes for the comfortable finger-lock first.

This is a physical illustration of how the brain naturally directs you towards what is most comfortable. We tend to repeat behaviour – sitting in the same chair, sleeping on the same side of the bed, always having the same meal in a restaurant – because it feels reassuring.

This might sound strange when applied to your fear, because you might not think that there is anything comfortable about having it. However, your brain thinks that changing so you can overcome your fear will be more uncomfortable than just living with it. The easiest course of action by far is just to do what we have done before. That's why people only change when they have decided they *want* to change.

The Great Black Things that have loomed against the horizon of my life, threatening to devour me, simply loomed and nothing more. The things that have really made me miss my train have always been sweet, soft, pretty, pleasant things of which I was not in the least afraid.

Elbert Hubbard

Our fears are a habit, and like any habit they are something we have practised. Whenever we try doing something that we don't normally do, our brains complain 'that's not me, that's not the way I do things'. Well, maybe up to now it hasn't been.

6. Now interlock your thumbs and fingers once again, and switch the position of your thumbs back and forth 15–20 times. As you keep changing them around you'll probably start to become aware that either way feels OK.

Choosing Change

Once you are committed to approaching things in a different way, change is possible.

An old farmer had plowed around a large rock in one of his fields for years. He had broken several plowshares and a cultivator on it, and had grown rather superstitious about the rock. After breaking another plowshare one day, and remembering all the trouble the rock had caused him through the years, he finally decided to do something about it. When he put a crowbar under the rock, he was surprised to discover that it was only about six inches thick and that he could break it up easily with a sledgehammer. As he was carting the pieces away he had to smile, remembering all the trouble that the rock had caused him over the years and how easy it would have been to have got rid of it sooner.

Think about your fear for a few moments as if it were that rock. Is it getting in the way of your life? Although you may have had your fear for a long time, that does not mean to say that you cannot remove it.

The key is in breaking the way you think about your fear and choosing to respond differently.

I've worked with people in the past who just want to talk about their problems and fears, and just go over and over them. Sometimes these people can be like mood hoovers, sucking all the good feelings out of you. They feel better because they've been able to talk about their fears, but if they are not prepared to *do* something about them, they'll never go away. Such people are addicted to focusing on the problem, rather than on what they are going to do about it.

If someone asked you 'What do you want to do about your fear?', what would you tell them? Would you tell them the history of your anxiety? Where it came from, and about all the times you've been frightened? I'm not saying it's wrong to talk about your fear, but doing something about it is the only way to change.

Becoming a Change Junkie

In order to get over your fear you need to get into the habit of experiencing change. The majority of people don't like change, even if it's to their benefit. But in order to free yourself from fear you're going to have to start doing things differently: Become a change junkie!

Anxiety and fear produce energy. Where we focus that energy noticeably affects the quality of our lives: Focus on the solution, not the problem.

Walter Anderson

Try doing as many things differently as you can. Travel to work a different way, sleep on the other side of the bed, eat different foods for a week, sit in a different chair.

You can change. Prove it to yourself in a number of small ways.

So What Do You Really Want?

It might surprise you to know that people often do not know what they want. For example, a person might say that they don't want to be frightened of heights, or they don't want to be scared on a plane. All the person is telling you is what they *don't* want, not what they *do* want.

Your anxieties and fears come from what your brain tells you about things, not from those things themselves. You attract what you focus on, and if you constantly think about your fear, that is what you will end up with. Instead of picturing what you do *not* want, you need to focus on what you *do* want.

Consider how you act when trying to achieve something. When you are booking a holiday, you don't tell the travel agent where you *don't* want to go. In the supermarket you don't amble up and down the aisles containing the foods you do not eat.

A friend once visited a hairdresser and was impressed when they gave her a form to complete asking her to detail all the sorts of cuts she disliked and definitely did not want. Having taken about 20 minutes to fill it in, she was confident of leaving with a style suited to her face and lifestyle. But because the focus of her consultation was on what she *didn't* want, and not what she did want, she still came away disappointed.

Positive thoughts (joy, happiness, fulfillment, achievement, worthiness) have positive results (enthusiasm, calm, well-being, ease, energy, love). Negative thoughts (judgment, unworthiness, mistrust, resentment, fear) produce negative results (tension, anxiety, alienation, anger, fatigue).

Peter McWilliams

A man came to see me and I asked him 'What do you want, how can I help you?' The guy replied he was anxious. As a child, his mother had locked him a cupboard when he behaved badly. I said, 'That's interesting, but what do you want? How can I help you?' 'Well,' he said, 'when I go into a room I get really nervous, I break out into a sweat, I go red and I don't know what to say to anyone, and usually I go home early because of this and then next time happens it's even worse.' I said, 'You are not telling me what you want, you are telling me how difficult it's been for you in the past. I am sympathetic to that, but I can't help you unless you can tell me what you want for yourself.' The man stopped for a second, surprised at this, and eventually replied that he didn't have the faintest idea, but he would think about it. Eventually he realized that what he wanted was to feel confident and interesting in social situations. I said: 'Can you imagine being those things?' He said he couldn't.

If we expect to change our behaviour we need to be able to imagine doing things differently, and we need to work out what we want to do differently. This is a new idea to many people, because we live in a society where people are focused on problems, transfixed by what is wrong, what is missing, what they haven't got. We are obsessed with the problems. We need to focus on solutions.

If we focus on the problem, or on how difficult things are, we make change impossible. We get what we focus on, and if you're obsessed with the problem you're going to find resolving it difficult.

How do you think good artists, architects, designers and hair-dressers get what they/their clients want? They have a clear vision of what they want to achieve. Rarely do they picture what they do *not* want to create. Instead they have a clear vision of what they want to achieve, and they set about creating it. How does a hairdresser cut your hair? Does she sit you down and say 'Don't tell me how you want your hair cut' and start cutting? Of course not. She talks with you about what you want, and makes a clear picture in her own mind of how your hair is going to look when it's finished. Does a builder start building a house by getting some bricks together? Of course not. A good builder will look at the architect's drawings; they will then work together to create the house they can see in their mind's eye. They engage all of their senses in the finished article. They can see the finished house long before they break the first clump of ground.

Once upon a time there were no toasters in the world. Somebody had the idea. They imagined it. They could see it. To them it was real, even though it only existed in the dimension of thought. If all you can see are your fears, how will you ever escape them? You have to shift your focus. Focus on what you want to happen, how you want to react.

Fear is static that prevents me from hearing myself.

Samuel Butler

What Do You Want?

a. Forget the problem – your fear – for a moment. Instead, ask yourself again what is it that you really want? Be specific. Do you want to be in control? Do you want to be relaxed? Do you want to be able to get on an aeroplane?

Do you want to be able to take a spider out of the bath?
Write it down here:

_____

_____

b. Now copy this down in large letters on a clean sheet of
    paper. You could stick it up somewhere where you will see
    it at least twice a day.
c. Even better, make a drawing of yourself having overcome
    your fear. You in control, feeling relaxed. It doesn't have to
    be a work of art.

**The process of focusing on the positive begins automatically to
eliminate the negative.**

I'm a great believer in writing things down and making pictures,
whatever it takes to shift your focus of attention.

I was once taking part in a workshop and the course leader
gave us all two minutes to write down ten things we wanted to
achieve in the next five to ten years. I jotted them all down. He
then said 'Look at each one and visualize yourself, as if in a
movie, having achieved these goals.' I didn't think that much of
it at the time, but eight years later I found this old notebook and
everything I'd written down had come true: writing books,
working with top athletes, having my own place to live, being
healthier.

So what do you think it takes to be successful on a big scale?
Is it some tremendous god-given talent? Is it luck or inherited
wealth? Is it genetics? Connections with the top people in your
field? Attitude? A decade of post-graduate education? It could
be any number of these things. Fortunately for most of us, what
it takes is something very simple and accessible: a clear vision.

This can be aided by making pictures, by writing things down, by creating clear mental visualizations of what you want to achieve. A study of Harvard graduates found that after 20 years, the 3 per cent of them who had written their goals down achieved more financially than the other 97 per cent combined. An average person with average talent, ambition and education can achieve great things if that person has clear, focused goals.

The process of writing things down is effective because it helps you create an image of what you want to achieve. One of your brain's greatest gifts is that it can help you in this. Have you ever been working on something and got stuck, gone away, then come back to find that the solution has emerged while you weren't actively thinking about it? The fact is, when you are clearly focused on something your brain works on it even when you are not consciously aware of it. Then, when parts of that vision arrive in your life, you are more likely to seize them.

What lies behind us and what lies before us are tiny matters compared to what lies within us.

Ralph Waldo Emerson

When I was 19 I experienced a health problem. The joint pain I was feeling meant I couldn't teach aerobics or play football. I rested, but the pain remained. I saw experts, I had injections. I was so obsessed with the problem, and not being able to do the things I wanted, that I became frightened, and worried about how long I was going to be out of action. I then went to a specialist who took an X-ray and a bone scan. He discovered a large gap in the pubic bone and wanted to wire it together. It would have meant a serious operation. When I thought about it I realized that I didn't want surgery. Instead, as a last resort, I tried acupuncture. The acupuncturist asked me what I wanted. I told him the history of the problem. He pointed to the door and said, 'That's a door. If you can't tell me what you want, I suggest you use it.' I realized that what I wanted was to have freedom of movement in my groin. As he treated me, he asked me to focus my thoughts on the times I had been able to run around. Three weeks later, my injury had gone. Was it the acupuncture, or was it the change in my focus that yielded results? The fact is that both approaches involved doing something different. I had been stuck in a rut, going to see doctors, accepting my fate, up until that moment when I realized that I had to help myself in a completely different way.

If you focus on how hard something is, or how hard you've tried in the past, or on how frightened you are, you won't be able to help yourself or free yourself from fear. Work out precisely what you want now.

Many people think change is difficult. They have been conditioned to believe that. But think of all the other times in your life when you have changed. The clothes you wear, the places you go and the things you talk about are probably vastly different now from what they were ten years ago. You made a transition, and going back to your past wardrobe, past hangouts or past conversations is unthinkable, maybe even unbearable. In many of these instances the change you made was not a struggle. The changes occurred consciously, or even unconsciously, without tears, fuss or effort.

Often people think they want to change some element of their behaviour, but can't work out why they don't seem to be able to find the motivation. Perhaps this is because they don't really actually want to change, or are trying to make themselves into someone they don't really want to be. A friend used to say she wished she were the kind of person who enjoyed baking, but could never work up the enthusiasm for trying it. It was only when she just had a go that she discovered how fun baking was for her. Thinking we *should* want something, and really *wanting* it, are two completely different things, just as thinking about something and actually doing it are.

Change won't happen until we're genuinely committed to it because we want it enough. Changes are usually difficult to make because the patterns of behaviour we follow are habits. And although many of our habits are positive, the sort of habits we want to change are the ones that can be destructive and damaging in the long term. We want to stop smoking, overeating, getting too little exercise. There is an element of denial necessary in changing any of the things we do because we like them. You won't get anywhere if you focus on what you are going to be missing. When you want to change something, you need to focus on the positive benefits of making the change.

It is not because things are difficult that we do not dare, it is because we do not dare that they are difficult.

Seneca

Looking on the Bright Side

Everyone knows that exercising is good for them, and everyone seems to enjoy the feeling, the natural high that we get when we finish, the sense of satisfaction and pleasure. But for a lot of people the thought of exercising is pretty negative: having to go to the gym, being around people who seem fitter and have better bodies, getting your hair wet. It is very easy to talk ourselves out of exercise. But for the next few weeks, become more active by focusing on the feeling you get when exercise is finished. And with that feeling in mind, go and exercise.

Focus

If you are not prepared to focus on making change, then chances are you are just going to go back to what you were doing before. As this book progresses, I'm going to give you plenty of suggestions for how to change your focus. Later on we'll learn about the power of visualizing colour, the importance of breathing, the power of trusting your own senses, and the benefits of giving yourself healthy positive thoughts.

Do you know how powerful thought is? If you focus on something, it's what you tend to get. If you throw something out it tends to reflect what comes back. I'm not religious, but the power of prayer has been proven in scientific studies. In one American study, people who were unwell and being prayed for recovered more quickly than those for whom no one was praying. Likewise, if you focus on someone and think well of them, your positive intention is more likely to help them. Having positive thoughts for yourself and for the people you know creates a space for good things to happen.

I often work with people who want to lose weight. If you ask them if they think it is difficult to lose weight, most people will say 'yes.' I always ask them 'why?' The answer: They tried in the past and it was difficult. But this doesn't automatically mean it will be difficult in the future. However, if you keep thinking about how hard it was last time you tried, you are already setting yourself up to fail.

Do not be too timid and squeamish ... All life is an experiment.
The more experiments you make, the better.

Ralph Waldo Emerson

When Thomas Edison embarked on his quest to invent the lightbulb, no lightbulbs existed. He tried countless approaches. One day, a journalist asked him how it felt to have failed so many times. Edison, surprised, answered, 'What do you mean? I've successfully found all these ways that don't work.' Edison realized that in order to get things right, they were going to have to go wrong first.

Fear of Fear Itself

Perhaps it's true to say that no one actually fears heights or change or the unknown, or whatever their particular brand of fear is. What they really fear is the out-of-control feeling they experience when confronted by these things. Take flying. The tendency is to focus on the plane. But it's nothing to do with the plane. The plane is a piece of welded aluminium or steel. The thing you need to confront is *yourself*. What terrified you is what the plane *represents* in your own mind.

What we need to change is our relationship to things we can't control. Risks will always be there. Life is one big risk from the moment we are born. People who call themselves 'nervous' or 'fearful' are choosing to be this way because they've been practising, often for years. Some people proudly declare 'I'm not a risk-taker.' Well, what on earth does that mean? Stop for a moment and think of the risks you've taken in your life. As a young child, you risked first standing up to walk. You risked eating new foods. Everything was an unknown quantity at that stage, but you welcomed new experience.

A New Language

We often do not realize that the words we use can radically affect how we feel about overcoming a fear.

1.   Think about the thing that creates your fear. Notice how you feel when you state that you are afraid to fly, or of spaces, or that group situations make you nervous. Chances are that just thinking about these situations brings on discomfort. What happens when people think about things that frighten them is that they start to imagine themselves in the fearful situation. It still fascinates me how many people I work with say that the *thought* of the thing that frightens them is worse than the reality. One woman came to see me who was terrified of flying. For weeks before a flight she went through hours of imagining the worst-case scenario. She was trapped in an endless disaster movie. But when I asked her to relate experiences of actually being on a plane, she told me, 'It really wasn't that bad.'

2. Now tell yourself that you *should* get over this fear. Take a moment to notice how you feel when you use the word 'should'. Do you feel particularly good?

3. What about 'ought to', 'need to', or 'must'? You are probably becoming aware that these words do not put you into an optimistic frame of mind. Instead of motivating you, they pile on the pressure.

4. Now try using some new words and phrases. Holding in mind the things you want, try saying 'I'm in control,' 'I'm going to fly,' 'I have good relationships.' Find the expression that gives you the best feeling. You might have to play around with this to find the right words for you, but that's OK. Which ones make you feel the best? Write them down _____

_____

I'm not asking you to find the words that will make you believe you can change, just the ones that make you feel good. Say the phrase that fits you best over and over to yourself, like you really mean it, whether or not you can truly believe it at this stage. These kinds of positive words and phrases are known as 'affirmations', and they can make a real difference in how you feel about yourself and whatever in your life you want to change for the better. They open up your mind so that, for example, you can make the first steps towards conquering your fears.

The death of fear is in doing what you fear to do.

Sequichie Comingdeer

Approaching Your Fear Differently

Our perception of things often makes us fearful – after all, we're not all scared of the same things. And we invest a lot of time and energy in our fears. This means that many of us start looking for things to prove our theories right. Our brains seek to reinforce our belief that we are right to be afraid, so we look for evidence to back it up. What do you think the chances are that someone who's always moaning that bad things keep happening to them is likely to find success? Or that a woman who declares 'all men are bastards' will find everlasting love? Focusing on what you *don't* want is an effective way of bringing it about.

How many couples do you know who have a genuinely great relationship? If you had an experience growing up in a family where your parents had a poor relationship you may have spent years observing them being unhappy, or sensing stress in the house. You possibly learned to be frightened of being hurt, of being betrayed or having someone cheat on you. But although your fear is supposed to protect you, it actually creates the very thing you fear. If you are in a relationship and are frightened of being hurt, you are more likely to behave in ways that generate a situation where you are hurt.

The Power of a Different Approach

The Englishman goes to France and he says to the Frenchman, 'Excuse me, where is the Eiffel tower?' The Frenchman says, 'Je ne comprends pas' ('I don't understand'). So the Englishman says, a bit louder this time, 'Where Is The Eiffel Tower?' Soon he's shouting 'WHERE IS THE EIFFEL TOWER?' Often we go along with the same approach when we should say to ourselves, 'Stop, try something different.' A slight adjustment in our attitude can make a big difference to results.

Have you ever seen a fly trapped in a room? It tries to get out by constantly flying around in the same direction and banging into the same window. But if it just stopped, took a deep breath, relaxed and looked around, it might notice the open door just inches away.

If someone has a fear they may go to great lengths to avoid it, which takes a lot of effort. But if instead they change the way they think about the fear, approaching it from another perspective, it immediately becomes easier to deal with.

We all have the ability to try different approaches, but as we get older we get stuck in our ways. We try the same approach over and over again, even though it doesn't work. What I'm trying to do in this book is to open all the doors and windows as wide as they will go. But in order to benefit, you need to stop what you're doing, consider a new perspective, and try a different direction.

Once upon a time there was a king who ruled a prosperous country. One day, he went on a trip to a distant part of his kingdom. When he got back to his palace he complained that his feet were sore because the road had been rough and stony. He then ordered that every road in the country be covered with leather. One of his wisest servants considered this, and dared himself to approach the king. 'Why do you have to spend that amount of money? Why don't you cut a little piece of leather and use it to cover your feet?'

To make the world a happier place to live in, you need to change yourself, not the world.

Practice easing your way along. Don't get het up or in a dither. Do your best; take it as it comes. You can handle anything if you think you can. Just keep your cool and your sense of humor.

Smiley Blanton, MD

What All Fears Have in Common

Fears are behaviours that you have learned. Because you have learned them, you can unlearn them.

Start to think of your brain as a computer. It absorbs information about what is going on around and inside you, it makes complex comparisons and decisions, and it issues instructions to the rest of the body about what to do. For example, if someone greets you and extends their hand in greeting, you are shaking hands before you've even realized it. You don't stop first and run through the other options – tickling their outstretched hand, staring at it or stroking it. In the same way, fear is like a software package that becomes hard-wired until it seems to be the only software you can use to interpret events. Every time you experience your fear, the outcome and your conclusions are the same. This will continue to happen until you start to see the situation in a different light.

The simple truth is: if you carry on doing what you have always done, the chances are you will continue to get the same results. What will really make your experience different is learning how to behave differently. The challenge Is to spring-clean the habits your brain has picked up throughout your life.

Ask yourself this: do you think you have a choice when deciding whether or not to accept the brain's instruction? You do, and you are not limited to doing what you have always done in the past.

A New Day, a New Start

Think of every day as a blank page. What you put on that page is entirely up to you. It's so easy to put the same as you did yesterday or the day before. But you don't have to if you don't like the way it makes you feel.

Most of us have had uncomfortable and frightening experiences in our lives, and we worry about these things happening again. But projecting this worry or fear into the future can stop us from enjoying our lives fully. It limits our potential. Worrying is a mechanism we put in place as a protection against being hurt, but it also prevents us from being completely free.

Chances are, your brain has created your fears because it is trying to protect you or look after you, or stop you getting hurt or even dying. Accept that this part of you has become very strong and can sometimes work automatically.

But perhaps it's working so hard that it has lost touch with what is really going on. Maybe it has actually started limiting you.

One of my clients was afraid of balloons. When she was two years old a big red balloon popped in her face and burned her lips. From that moment on, whenever she saw a balloon she became extremely frightened that history would repeat itself. Now in her twenties, she was very careful to avoid balloons. In fact, when she thought she might be going to a place where there might be balloons, her mind automatically conjured up a way of frightening her. She would envision 50-foot tall red balloons coming towards her. As they got closer and closer she thought she was going to die. Adrenaline was released into her bloodstream, she felt physically fearful because, in her mind, the balloons threatened her survival. You can understand why she would avoid them at all costs. She learned very quickly, in that split second when she was tiny, to be frightened of balloons and loud noises. She thought balloons meant pain, so her mind conjured up her fear to help her. But it was misguided in this.

Do the things/You believe in/In the name of love/And know that/ You aren't alone/We all have doubts and fears.

Carole King

Your body follows what your brain tells it to do. How many of your everyday thoughts are new, and how many are old ones that you have repeated for as long as you can remember? Each time you repeat a thought you reinforce its power, and the circuit or pathway along which you think gets stronger, leaving less room for new and empowering, creative ideas.

One of the most common elements of people who have fears is the negative communication they have with themselves. This is what some people call 'internal dialogue'.

One of the ways in which you can stop your fear is to be aware that, despite believing you have no control over it, you *do* have control over what you are *saying* to yourself.

You can make the choice to stop attacking yourself with negative thoughts by becoming your own 'thought-coach'.

Creating Your Inner Coach

A friend worked with a very famous French football player and asked him, 'Are you aware of your internal dialogue?' The Frenchman didn't really understand, and my friend thought the translation had confused him, so he asked again, 'Can you hear different voices in your head, telling you what to do?' The Frenchman got more confused, but eventually he said: 'Ahh ... you mean zee duck in my 'ead.' My friend was a bit perplexed by now, thinking he had confused them both, but the footballer went on to describe the duck in his head that put negative thoughts in his mind.

Now, I don't know if every French football player has a duck in his head, but everyone certainly has a voice in their head, talking to them all the time, so my friend said to the player, 'Well, have you ever thought of getting the duck to shut up, even saying to the duck, "shut the duck up"?'

If you give the judgemental, worrying voices in your head a command to be quiet, that's exactly what will happen. It's a simple way to put yourself in a state that allows you to begin to focus on what's really going on underneath all the background noise. Practise this.

Just as when you were a child and had an imaginary friend or pet, or would imagine you were a doctor, nurse or fireman, I want you to create your own inner coach. Your coach's responsibility is to take care of you, look after you, be gentle, positive and encouraging at all times.

Take a moment to decide what sort of voice you would like your inner coach to have. Is it a motivational coach? Or perhaps it sounds sexy and seductive like Barry White? Maybe it has a strong Yorkshire accent. Don't be bound by gender or age. You can create the inner coach of your dreams, the one who will make you feel great. The important thing is that the voice should be empowering and reassuring. You could write it all out, creating a character, scripting a personality. Play around with it.

Remember, this coach has no ego, he or she just wants you to get the best out of yourself. Your coach is gentle and considerate and kind, never critical. He or she is your best friend, there to represent your best interests, and flows from your heart, not your head.

We'll work with this image throughout the book, but you can start working with your inner coach yourself on a daily basis: Whenever you start to hear negative thoughts voiced in your mind, imagine your inner coach getting to work, stamping out worries about what you feel – getting the duck to shut up. If you feel nervous or stressed, let your inner coach remind you to take a deep breath or encourage you to focus on something else. Remember, this is not opening night, you don't have to perfect it immediately. Work on it.

If the fearful, critical part of you starts up, let your inner coach put things back into perspective with some reassuring words or by suggesting something to do that you enjoy. Start to become responsible for how you treat yourself.

The most drastic and usually the most effective remedy for fear is direct action.

William Burnham

Stop Focusing on a World of Fear

You may believe that you can't overcome your fear because you've tried in the past and it hasn't worked. You may believe that you can't because your fear seems to be such a big part of your life and defines, in part, who you are. You may believe that you can't succeed because confronting your fear will involve pain and discomfort.

If you want to master your fear, shift your focus away from it. Focus instead on what you will gain from losing your fear.

Whenever you find yourself worrying, ask yourself these questions and let the answers play over and over in your head:

⊘ What would it feel like to overcome my fear?
⊘ What would be different?
⊘ How much better would I feel?

If you believe that you can master your fear, you are right! Equally, if you believe that you can't master it, you're also right. Can't equals won't. Did you know that one of the functions of your brain is to confirm what you believe? For example, if you believe that you are fat, the chances are you will act like a fat person, eating more than you need to, moving as if you are carrying a lot of excess weight (even if you're not), and being inactive. If you believe that you are shy, then again, your actions will reflect that belief.

But you weren't born fat, you weren't born shy, and you weren't born with your fear. Your fears and anxieties are just things that you have learned. If there are things that you say to yourself that mean you can't, now is the time to dump them.

Exercise: 'I Can't' Funeral

Take a sheet of paper and write 'I can't ... ' at the top of the page. Now write down the negative messages that you give yourself. For example, 'I can't socialize because I'm boring.' 'I can't catch a ball because I've got butter fingers.' 'I can't find the right partner because I'm shy.' 'I can't find happiness because I'm just not that sort of person.'

When you have written down your list of self-limiting beliefs, scrunch up the sheet of paper and either throw it away or burn it. As you do so, get your inner coach to repeat the following affirmation: 'I no longer need to believe there are things I can't do. I can do anything I choose to do. All I need to know is that change is possible and can become a reality as soon as I want it to.'

If you stop believing that you can't, it gives space for you to start to think you can.

You can break your reliance on fearful thoughts by thinking about what you stand to gain by losing them.

Imagine, in your mind's eye, a film about how you want things to be. Watch yourself, then imagine stepping into the film yourself. It might not turn out exactly the way you picture it, because other people are unknown factors, but there is one thing that you definitely can control: your own mind.

Learn to control the controllable, and let the rest take care of itself.

Change your thoughts, you change the world.

Norman Vincent Peale

3

Why Am I Afraid?

How We Learn Fear

Hesitation, depression or envy of those who appear to have what we want are often signs of weakness or lack of vigorous, clear purpose. These feelings may be saying we're not yet ready to create our own good. When we're emotionally unprepared, we want something for nothing, and quickly.

Marsha Sinetar

Many of our fears have been with us from an early age, and many of them have come about from copying or mimicking the people around us. When you are a baby, no one gives you a manual telling you how to get the best from your brain. You simply copy what you see in an unfamiliar world.

As babies and children we absorb almost everything that happens around us, soaking up everything like a sponge. But because we have no way of discerning what is valuable, useful fears can get muddled up with unproductive fears. We have no specific mechanism with which to filter all the incoming information; we just watch and learn particular behaviours without knowing at the time which will prove useful and which not. All we know when we are young is how to copy and imitate what we see.

We learn things in two ways: through our own senses, and by example. When we learn through our own sensory experiences as children we are learning first-hand.

When we learn through copying, on the other hand, we can absorb behavioural and emotional prejudices which are of little value to us – and as we usually have no way of assessing this at the time, we may spend the rest of our lives living by these redundant rules.

So, a child who watches his parents react negatively every time a spider is around observes this behaviour and learns how to respond the same way. The child thinks this is the correct way to behave around spiders, and carries on being frightened. In fact, he gets better and better at being frightened as time goes on. Soon this fear response becomes an imprint and the process is no longer thought about – a habit has been established.

Children tend to be curious about the world they live in. For example, imagine a small child peering around his mother's legs at grandma's cat. Is this child curious or scared? The child may be fascinated by glimpses of the animal as his mother moves from foot to foot. But it would also be reasonable to interpret the child's response as fear of the cat. If this is how the child's actions are perceived, then this is how she will be treated. If an adult then reaches down to comfort her, the child may think that this is a frightening situation, and start to associate similar situations with being afraid. At the extreme, the child could become scared of cats, even though she has never been hurt by one.

If your father hit your mother, you had no idea whether that was right or wrong. You would just accept that this was how grown-ups are. It would come to seem normal to you.

Perhaps your father refused to walk under ladders. He seemed fearful of the consequences of this; clearly, something nasty was obviously going to happen to him if he did. Without realizing it, you would most likely inherit his superstition and develop a fear of walking under ladders, even though you had had absolutely no direct experience that such activity leads to trouble. Some people are superstitious about putting up an umbrella indoors, seeing a magpie, or letting a black cat cross their path. These beliefs haven't existed since the beginning of time. They are the result of learned behaviour being passed down to each successive generation. That we can be so affected by them demonstrates the power of conditioning.

Superstitions give us more rocks to navigate around, more things to be frightened of. There are enough rocks in life without making them up.

Your fears and anxieties are just behaviours that you have learned, possibly in a very similar way to this. Every time you experience something that frightens you, you come to the same conclusions, continuing to programme yourself to believe that a fearful reaction is the *only* way to react. Your brain tends to suggest ways that it thinks are the best ways, and these responses have been practised by you to the point that you can respond with fear automatically.

As we grow up we are encouraged to follow the rules of our culture, and the values of our family. Our brains are being shaped by modes of acceptable behaviour passed down from parents, through education and by religion. Our reactions and our perspectives on life are automatically filtered through the things we experience and absorb, from childhood onwards. The trouble is that much of this shaping is imposed on us by the use of scare tactics: 'If you don't hand your homework in on time your teacher will be cross.' 'If you don't do as you're told you won't get any Christmas presents.' 'If you don't say your prayers you won't go to heaven.'

In between goals is a thing called life that has to be lived and enjoyed.

Sid Caesar

Through sheer repetition, we learn to accept our parents' values, definitions and rules as correct. This is not to blame anyone, it's just that our experiences create our world. Chances are, your parents were trying to do the best they could. Nevertheless, what you need to understand is that you can transcend any of their outdated or no longer useful messages or warnings, definitions and rules – because you have the power to change.

Having had a less than perfect past does not condemn you to an imperfect future. But some of us get stuck in the past. But one of the best things about the past is that it's over.

Because you have learned your fearful reaction, you can unlearn it. You need to replace your fear with a more positive behaviour which enables you to think and act in a more self-nourishing way.

You can develop your own 'user manual' that will allow you to break any unwanted fears and live the life you want to lead. You can learn to control fear, rather than let it control you.

Why Am I Afraid to Tell You Who I Am?

Many people find it hard to find the right balance between their need to be an individual and conforming socially. Many of us are taught that it's important to be part of a group and to fit into society, and yet at the same time we are taught the benefits of being self-sufficient.

Once in the group we are expected to act in a certain way, but the more we do this the more we deny our true selves, and the more we stop examining what we are feeling. Soon we are numbed. I've worked with smokers who want to quit their habit, but are scared that quitting will leave them feeling alienated from their friends. They don't have much of a chance of giving up their habit when their fear of being socially isolated is greater than their desire to stop. If you flaunt your individuality, you risk isolation. But giving up on yourself in order to conform can also be unfulfilling. The solution is to understand that you have choices.

From my experience with clients and in my own life, I've realized that people are often struggling to be themselves, yet are frightened that if they express their own ideas or attitudes then perhaps they won't be liked. Just how many people who are famous are never really themselves? Putting on an act, many of them are terrified that if people see them for who they really are they will be rejected.

The greatest mistake you can make in life is to continually fear you will make one.

Elbert Hubbard

Our early world is defined and determined by the people around us. Most babies and young children get plenty of attention, and believe that their parents exist only to care for them. As we grow older, however, we discover that the people around us can become absorbed in something or someone other than us. This, at first, feels like being abandoned. We experience rejection. We learn that we can go from being the centre of attention to being just one distraction among many, competing for love and affection.

Some people react to this by becoming vulnerable and frightened. They may blame themselves, and come to believe that they are somehow unacceptable.

They then set off into life looking for this belief to be confirmed, because it has become fundamental to their understanding of themselves and the world. Rather tragic when you think about it.

Once you've learned to think that there is something wrong with you, this belief is very powerful. What it means is that shame or guilt becomes part of your identity; you can't imagine not feeling like this. And these feelings can underscore everything you do. Stepping back from what you do and trying to take yourself less seriously, and understanding that you are more than the sum of your guilts or fears, and that everyone has these feelings, can help.

Breakout: Why Do I Feel So Alone?

If you were trapped in a car and the car was on fire, you wouldn't watch the flames and inhale the smoke. Your instinct would be to get out of there as fast as possible. The adrenaline pumps and you flee. In a life-threatening situation it's very rare to stand still. Your brain is engineered to protect you. You have grown up knowing that fire and smoke can kill you. It's a strong, clear conviction that you share with everyone else.

In a case such as this of a clear external danger, you can be certain that other people will understand how you feel. But not all fears are universally felt. When your fear is specific to you, it can be very difficult to communicate it to anyone else. It can be difficult for other people to understand, because they are not experiencing what you are experiencing. Although we all have fears of one sort or another, if no one else seems to understand our specific fears, we come to feel shame, anxiety and guilt about having them or trying to express them.

Human beings have a greater consciousness and ability to think abstractly than any other animal. It's a gift, but it can also be a burden, because it enables us to realize that we are entirely alone in our heads. We can only reach other people through communicating with them. No one can step into our brains. We are, in this very real sense, completely alone. I've worked with people who cling to what they know because they fear that without external values there will be no structure to hold them together. They don't realize that countless other people experience the aloneness of being a human being. As a child if you found yourself in a situation filled with pain or anger, you could scream, and your parents would come rescue and comfort you. Most people want to be able to give themselves this same kind of protection, but don't know where to start.

Life is a grindstone. Whether it grinds us down or polishes us up depends on us.

Thomas L. Holdcroft

The Fear We Need

Fear is an integral part of our makeup. Consider our distant ancestors: they needed fear for their survival – if there was a sabre-tooth tiger stalking them across the savannah they needed to be able to get away, fast. Although there aren't any sabre-tooth tigers at the bottom of our gardens, there are times in our lives when responding to situations fearfully is appropriate. There are also many more times when you have learned to be frightened of things that there is no need to fear.

Babies and toddlers don't understand the danger of water, or traffic, or heights. They require constant observation and care because their fearless nature can very easily prove fatal. We put gates across the stairs to prevent them exploring quite so fearlessly. We take particular care when they are near water to prevent the tragic consequences of their fearless curiosity. We never let them outside alone.

As our brains are being wired up in the first few years of life, a fear reflex kicks in. If we trip or hurt ourselves, we release the hormone adrenaline. Soon, this fight-or-flight chemical can be triggered by the suggestion that we might be about to hurt ourselves. A surge of this chemical gives us the focus and strength to remove ourselves from a potentially dangerous situation. Fear is the emotion that makes your heart jump as you get an instantaneous adrenaline surge – from a small dose that leads to churning butterflies in response to a minor threat to your well-being, to a powerful dose that jolts you to flee.

The Chemistry of Fear

Fear is an emotion that stems from several hormonal and neuro-chemical responses in the brain. Adrenaline is released, which increases heart rate and respiration, a process known as the 'fight or flight response'. These symptoms are meant to stay active for just a few moments or minutes, giving you just enough time to react to the object of the fear. The problems happen when that object is not real – there is no lion, tiger or bus bearing down on you – but instead you are worrying about something created in your mind. In this case, your body suffers for a much longer period of time under the effects of high levels of adrenaline. Your heart keeps pumping nervously, you can't settle, you have an impercep-tible sense of worry that is very stressful. And because there is no external threat to confront or avoid, it is difficult to imagine that you can ever escape from the controlling grasp of these uncom-fortable and damaging feelings.

What Is Adrenaline?

Adrenaline is a natural internal stimulant that creates feelings of intensity. It is a hormone secreted by part of the brain called the *adrenal medulla* in response to stress. When it is released in the body it can produce many forms of intensity. We are free to interpret those effects how we choose. We may experience the presence of adrenaline as excitement or fear.

Adrenaline stimulates the heart, raises blood pressure, constricts the surface vessels and dilates lung capacity. It also boosts the available blood sugar, increasing immediate levels, while depleting the reserves. This gives us an immediate burst of energy.

With a surge of adrenaline in our bodies we are prepared, by nature, to fight or to flee. Our heart rate and lung capacity are increased. Our sensitivity to pain is reduced and our awareness of less essential emotions is repressed.

It is very liberating to realize that feeling fear does not mean you are in danger. But unfortunately it may take very little to trigger a fear reaction in your body. This fear emotion causes adrenaline to rush through your bloodstream. The more adrenaline, the more fear you feel – even if there is no reason to feel it.

What's more, adrenaline is a highly addictive substance. It is closely related to methamphetamine – commonly called speed – and its impact on the brain is the same. Living for long periods with the fear chemical – adrenaline – coursing around our bodies in low doses has actually made us addicted to these feelings.

As we grow older, some limited experience of the sort of situations that trigger the production of adrenaline helps our brains to develop a vitally important form of fear that is as crucial to our survival as food and water. It's a rational, animalistic, instinctive fear that we all have. It's a real gift. It keeps us alive.

If you didn't develop the capacity to feel this primal fear there would be nothing to stop you jumping off tall buildings or wandering in front of traffic. It's an internal survival safeguard for when our parents are no longer able to supervise our every waking hour. We need it.

However, there is a drawback to this evolutionary benefit. Our brains are very good at producing the fear hormone – even when our survival is *not* threatened. This means we can end up producing an adrenaline response in situations where it hinders, rather than helps us.

An adrenaline surge can be very draining, even though your body usually produces the response for just a brief moment of time.

In a way I can't help but marvel at people who live with a lot of fear, because sustaining fear at this kind of level is hard work. People who are perpetually frightened invest a lot of time in feeling that way. What they don't realize sometimes is that they are *choosing* to do so.

Facing up to the fact that some parts of your life are ruled by fear is the first important step to conquering it. Fear exerts a powerful influence over us. Admitting this to yourself can be hard. Fear can lead us to work too hard, or become bad-tempered, to drink too much or, at an extreme, to become ill and depressed. All these behaviours are means we use to ensure we can hide this weakness, our fear, from ourselves.

Do not waste worry. If you're going to worry, worry well. Put that energy to good use; aim it at an answer. Don't forget: Nothing diminishes anxiety faster than action.

Walter Anderson

What I would like you to do is to set aside how you feel about whatever it is that you fear. I am going to encourage you to use your awareness and your senses to consider an alternative reality. You can learn more about something by looking at it in more than one way.

Courageous people don't deny fear; they acknowledge it and face it. Fear exists to help our survival. It's an ally, a magic force, that lives within all of us and which helps us to transcend ourselves in moments of danger.

However, making the distinction between survival fear and unnecessary fear is not always easy – a habitual fear in some circumstances is perfectly appropriate. If flying into a storm or easing into busy traffic isn't the right time to get a little scared, then when is? If you are in a situation such as walking down a dark alley and you hear footsteps behind you, it's natural to feel some fear. You want your brain to be able to recognize these potential dangers.

Breakout: Why Is Fear So Exhausting?

When you see danger and act immediately – either striking out or running away – your body mobilizes itself very quickly and effectively into protective action. Your heart-rate increases rapidly so you can take in more oxygen. Large quantities of the hormone adrenaline, are released into the bloodstream for delivery to your muscles. Blood flow is drawn away from non-essential areas (such as the digestive system and the surface of the skin) as blood is diverted to your brain and muscles. Whatever you decide to do, your body is prepared for action.

But if you decide to do nothing, this is where things become very unpleasant. It's enormously exhausting to be constantly in this state of adrenaline-fuelled arousal. If you live like this for too long without taking action, you are inviting a cycle of fear where these churning feelings become normal. Instead of putting your fear into action to create a result, you are living the fear every day.

How Fear Can Damage Your Health

Fear and anxiety lead to stress. When you are stressed, adrenaline drips into the system. When you live like this long term you do great physical harm to your body. Forced to remain in situations that produce stress, your metabolism changes. The human body is simply not constructed to constantly operate on emergency power. Long-term exposure to low levels of adrenaline leads to disorders such as hypertension, and to alcohol and substance abuse as means of 'coping'. Over-exposure can lead to loss of appetite, insomnia, fatigue, loss of libido, Irritable Bowel Syndrome and a general decline in health.

Adrenaline harms our immune systems, contributes to heart disease and helps in the development of cancers. A long-term study of 400 male and 200 female executives – people who routinely operate under high levels of adrenaline – showed that the men suffered more heart problems and the women more cancer than people who had less stressful, anxiety-causing jobs.

WHAT IS STRESS?

Stress is a state when any demand is placed on the nervous system. This includes almost every event – travelling to a new place, eating new food, being in cold weather. It is the *level* of stress in our lives, and how we *react* to it, that determines whether it is healthy or unhealthy.

Long-term stress comes from attitudes and emotions associated with the future as well as the past. This can keep your stress levels high and your tolerance low. It causes us to spend a lot of time and energy keeping our daily stress level tolerable, or leads us to be stressed out all the time. We can cope with this sort of stress if we get over each event like a little blip in our stress levels. The danger comes when we add all these problems together.

Panic stress is caused by a sudden unexpected stimulus. We are subjected to a sudden bolt of fear as adrenaline floods our system in a bid to protect us from a traffic accident or a physical attack.

Sometimes when we talk about being stressed, we actually mean we feel anxious. The word 'anxiety' comes from an old Indo-European word *angh*. From the beginning, anxiety has referred to a terrifying inner state, rather than an actual outer danger. Anxiety and fear are related to each other, but a great deal of confusion exists regarding the difference between them. Fear has become a catch-all category, and is the most commonly used term in English. We talk about having a fear of flying or commitment, yet phobias are also referred to as fears, which can be confusing. According to the psychologist Robert Gerzon: 'Fear originally meant a calamity or disaster, later it came to mean the emotion triggered by such catastrophic events. Over the centuries the word "fear" has come to mean almost any negative emotion including anxiety, agitation, apprehension, worry, nervousness, depression, grief, dread, terror and panic.

When Is a Fear a Phobia?

Many people think that they have a phobia, but in fact they haven't. What most people term a phobia is actually just a fear that they have practised. A lot of people think they have a phobia of spiders or snakes, but it's much more likely that they are just very frightened of them. This is a primal response to things which in our past were a genuine threat. We are fearful of spiders, heights, the dark – things which our ancestors would have felt as a threat. Smoking and driving kill far more people in today's world, but its very rare to find someone who is afraid of cigarettes or cars.

A true phobic reaction is a whole different category of terror, a central nervous wildfire that's impossible to mistake. The distinction between a fear and a phobia is extent and intensity. True phobias are always on the mind of the phobic: these are compulsive thoughts that consume every waking moment. Real phobias overtake the dynamics of personality.

If you think you may be phobic, I strongly recommend you seek professional support.

The good news is that you are probably not phobic. It is much more likely that sometimes you are frightened. This is good news. When your worry is fear-based, rather than due to phobic behaviour, it is much easier to overcome. Your fear is happening inside your mind. You have great control over your mind, and can do whatever you want with it. All the resources you need are inside you.

REDUCING STRESS AND ANXIETY IN OUR LIVES

One of the most useful ways we can reduce stress and anxiety in our lives is to use the under-used right side of our brain. In the West, we tend to operate almost exclusively out of our logical, left brain. We try to control everything, manipulate circumstances and predict the future. This leads inevitably to stress and anxiety, because life doesn't always cooperate. If you keep focusing on trying to control things that are outside your control, there comes a point when there is nothing left and you are completely drained.

Using your creative right brain can help you make the stress in your life much more manageable. Encourage yourself to practise unconditional love, to do your best, do what you think is right – and let the results take care of themselves. Instead of trying to control the outside world, focus on your inner space. Give yourself enjoyable experiences, sleep, listen to music, exercise, and eat healthily.

Attitude Is All

A 23-year study by American scientists, the first long-term investigation to compare people's attitudes to ageing and how long they live, has reported that – in the words of Dr Becca Levy, the lead researcher of the Yale University report – 'Negative self-perceptions can diminish life expectancy; positive self-perceptions can prolong life expectancy.' Having a positive attitude and outlook definitely helps people as they age. Those who take up new challenges and are prepared to take on new ideas are more likely to be healthy.

For the next few weeks, stop focusing on what other people think and get your inner coach to help you to be more responsible on just being you, on being happy and excited about your life.

Controlling the Controllables

It is important to remember that the world is full of uncontrollable things. Even if we feel healthy and secure, we can't prevent illness, injury or death. We *can*, however, change the way we deal with the unknown.

Our thoughts literally build the world we see, heading us either towards happiness and success or unhappiness and failure. The great thing to remember is that *you are in control*. Some of the open, childlike qualities that you still possess will enable you to conquer your unproductive fears for good.

To acquire knowledge, one must study; but to acquire wisdom, one must observe.

Marilyn vos Savant

Own Your Fear

If there were no difficulties, there would be no triumphs.

Anon

Many people are frightened to admit that they need help. They are frightened to show their 'weakness'. They are frightened of losing control, or frightened of what they might find out about themselves.

Sportspeople are a great example of what happens if you don't address your fears: they surface when you're at your most vulnerable. A golfer I worked with had a fundamental fear that he wasn't good enough. When he played people whom he perceived to be worse than himself, he played well. However, whenever he was playing someone he thought was better than him, he was filled with fear and self-doubt. What he needed was his own inner coach, like the one you have now, getting him to focus not on the opposition, but on himself. Getting him to control the controllables; encouraging him to breathe deeply and enjoy what he was doing. Golf is not a team sport, it's just you, the golf club, the ball and the course. The opposition is only actually in your mind. If you can master all the elements of the game, you can win. To win, what you need to control is within your control. But give the other player control over your mind and you are much less likely to win.

Fear of Commitment

Whatever you do, you need courage.

Ralph Waldo Emerson

The first fear you learn is fear of abandonment. It's one of children's biggest fears, that they are going to be separated from their parents either intentionally or by accident. They hear the words 'You'll be the death of me' or 'I can't stand your behaviour any longer' and they panic. Maybe they lose sight of their mother in the shopping centre one day, and this leaves them feeling very afraid.

This fear of abandonment can have a massive impact on the whole of our lives. From our earliest moments of life we need and rely on others. Take them away and we feel incomplete. As we get older we learn that other people can choose to reject us. Because that's very painful, many of us try to protect ourselves by becoming very careful about what we say and do. We start thinking about what we are saying before we say it, just in case we are rejected for admitting who we really are.

Andrew, 36, says:

Although I do have an interest in finding the perfect partner, this is in conflict with a very strong part of my personality which adores the freedom and independence of being single. The idea of having a relationship makes me feel trapped. I worry about having to negotiate time for myself, my activities and my interests. I'm worried that the relationship might smother my enthusiasm for doing things that are challenging. A good relationship is comfortable, but makes me feel I'm at risk of forgetting who I am as a routine becomes established. For me, time spent on something new, something that challenges me to change or learn, is time well spent. So far, I haven't worked out how to maintain that in a relationship.

I have fallen in love very intensely in the past, only to find that my partner and I were completely incompatible, so I don't trust the feeling as a good judge of compatibility. Unfortunately this makes me rather cynical about love. It just seems safer when there's a choice to walk away, which is not to say that I do always walk away.

My greatest fear is being made to feel guilty for not loving the other person enough; being manipulated by the emotional needs of somebody else. I'm somebody who easily feels a sense of responsibility. Even though I have worked hard to understand this fear, it hasn't gone away. As a teenager I was rather under-confident and other people's approval was important to me. In the past I was attracted to women who were emotionally dependent because I imagined that somehow I could 'save' them; in return I would receive their approval. But any relationship based on partners not being at ease with themselves is unlikely to succeed.

I think one of the reasons I've tended not to start relationships, even when I've met someone potentially very nice, is the dream of finding the perfect partner. Maybe I'm addicted to having all the choices, but I'm worried about investing in one person and then somebody even more suitable coming along.

I'm actually fairly celibate. I find sex very powerful emotionally, and much that I'd like to think it can be separated from my emotions, I find that for me it can't, and that at heart I wouldn't want it to be.

I used to feel vulnerable if I'd had sex with someone; I was worried about being accused of being 'a typical male', so I went a bit too far the other way and became the sort of man who was unthreatening to women. I do want to leave behind this pattern of being the non-threatening male as a way of getting women's approval. I have good self-esteem now, but the idea of a relationship still makes me nervous, perhaps because I haven't yet met someone who inspires me enough to overcome the fear of my loss of independence.

Recently I had a conversation with a strongly emotional woman at a party. I was telling her about sailing and the role it has in my life, and how any partner of mine would feel second-best to the weather. She was trying to persuade me that a good relationship was enough to make all problems disappear. Her message that to be in love was everything, that nothing else matters, I fundamentally do not believe. In fact, I believe that the feelings of being in love carry a risk because they can obscure the importance of doing one's own activities. I feel so wonderful when I'm sailing; it is my focus, the ultimate source of my well-being and self-esteem. It's not about control, because you can't control the weather, but it is intensely satisfying when everything goes well. Having a relationship under these conditions would be a recipe for conflict.

In the past I would ask 'Is this person compatible with me?' I now realize the question is 'Am I compatible with a relationship?' I could meet the most perfect partner in the world, but the relationship would fail if I wasn't ready to be in one. And as things stand, I don't think I'm ready.

Pete says:

The only thing you came into life with was yourself. You didn't know about relationships, apart from those with your mother and father. In your earliest years you definitely did not need to have a relationship to have any degree of self-worth.

Being one-half of an adult sexual relationship is something that we are taught to value because it is highly prized by our culture. But stop and think about how few people you know who are truly happy and fulfilled in their relationship. Chances are, not that many. The reason for this is that the most precious thing you'll ever own in your life is your own space. Unfortunately, too many people try and share their lives with someone else before they have a real sense of their own space, and because they have so many insecurities of their own. They lose their space because they give it up in a misguided belief that this is what a successful rela-tionship requires. But this is why so many relationships break down. If you don't deal with your own insecurities they will just surface in the relationship. It's always important to make sure you have your own space and don't give that up, because this will only lead to feelings of frustration and hinder the relationship.

A good relationship is possible, but too many people embark on a love affair while still laden down with insecurities and imperfec-tions they haven't begun to address. Love is not blind, it is only a smoke screen, and sooner or later the smoke will clear. It's then that problems manifest themselves.

A lot of people misguidedly think that if they are in a relationship, then everything will be OK. This is the 'love conquers all' approach that Andrew has come up against. He is right to question this belief. The idea that your self-worth lies in being bonded with a partner is just a social construct. Andrew is being bold and strong, but he is still picking up messages from his friends and family that say 'it's wrong to be on your own'. Our culture puts a great deal of pressure on us to conform, think and act in certain ways. He is demonstrating great strength in ignoring those pressures, but nevertheless he continues to think there is something wrong with him because he's not conforming to social expectations.

You know when you just get stressed to the point where you are desperate for a holiday, or to be alone for a while? This is all about needing some space for yourself. Often we don't act on these feelings because they make us feel socially inept. Personal space is not something that our culture has taught us to value, but it is actually the most important element in a good relationship.

Andrew is frightened of commitment because he is aware that his sense of his own space is fragile. He also knows it is the most precious thing he will ever own. When he is sailing, his sense of his own space is at its strongest. But it is at its weakest when faced with the demands of a needful partner. Andrew is not ready to have a relationship, but he's not far off.

Being emotionally self-sufficient, and sharing your space with someone who is also this way, is a wonderful experience. But if you feel that your own sense of space is fragile, it can be a frightening prospect.

To increase your sense of space when you are in a relationship you must make time for yourself. Do things for yourself that you enjoy. This could be anything from going for walks to playing sport, having nights out with other friends – anything that makes you feel good and helps you to enjoy your life.

Whenever you feel you are losing sight of who you are, put your right hand on your chest, your left hand on top of it and breathe deeply from your stomach. Feel the solidity of your existence.

Andrew has made some really important realizations through his experience of being in relationships. He has learned that his own space is very precious. He's fighting the fear that needing this space is selfish. But why shouldn't he go sailing when he likes? The right partner for him would be someone who would recognize the nourishing power of his passion for sailing, and who would encourage him to go sailing as and when he wanted. He is right to accept nothing less.

Until you make peace with who you are, you'll never be content with what you have.

D. Mortman

The best sort of relationship you can have is when you want to share your life with someone, not become someone's life. But this requires that you actually have your own life, and that you find someone who is similarly sorted out. This is a challenge, because many people allow themselves to be ruled by their insecurities, but it's not impossible.

Andrew is fearful of being manipulated because this has happened to him in the past. He is the kind of person who tries to make everything better for the woman he is with. But he has learned a valuable lesson: You can't rescue anyone. And you can only change yourself.

This is a common reason why people are fearful of commitment. They have had experiences in the past when they felt they were forced to become more committed than they wanted to be, or they felt manipulated into behaving in a certain way by their partner. If you have been in a relationship in the past where you feel you have been abused or manipulated, you *allowed* someone to do that to you. By allowing it to happen, you were actually abusing yourself. Understanding this can give you the power to treat yourself better next time around.

A beautiful, nourishing relationship is one where you don't 'need' the other person and they don't 'need' you, but you just want to live your lives together, wanting each other to be happy and enjoy life. It's difficult, but it can be done. We don't need a relationship in life to feel whole, but we might *choose* to have one.

Unlike any viral or bacterial illness, fear can be caught over the telephone, from reading newspapers, or from watching television.

Peter McWilliams

What Do You Really Need?

What do you really need in your life? Make a list of all the things you need to feel happy and survive:

_____

_____

In fact, you only need water, food and warmth. You don't need a fast car, a fabulous home – or a relationship, although you may want these things. Would you be able to survive without a fast car or a relationship? Of course. Learn to recognize the difference between needs and wants.

The most important thing you can ever want is to feel comfortable with who you are. It is only by choosing to find ways to take care of the most important person in the world, yourself, that you have a chance to enjoy the rest of your life.

Do you need people to like you, or to have lots of money? These things might make you feel better about yourself, but only if you already have confidence and faith in who you are.

If you believe your life is only complete if you are in a relationship, if having a relationship feels like a need, not a want, then what you really need is to spend some time on your own, getting to know yourself. The best thing you can do for yourself is to have a break, particularly if you have a history of broken or difficult relationships. Work on your own independence. Take care of yourself. It's a very big step to take responsibility for yourself, but it is the route to happiness. You might have had a difficult relationship with your parents; you may have had bad experiences which have affected your life. But these things do not have to be part of your future. You are the only person holding you back. Take responsibility for your life. Own your own fear.

If you want a nourishing relationship, allow yourself to remain open to the fact that there might be someone out there with whom you want to share your life. If you are fearful of commitment, stop believing that commitment is necessary for happiness and allow yourself to accept that it's fine to be alone. People who define their existence by an intense need to be in a relationship, or by a similarly intense fear of commitment, tend to attract the wrong sort of people into their lives.

Difficult times have helped me to understand better than before, how infinitely rich and beautiful life is in every way, and that so many things that one goes worrying about are of no importance whatsoever.

Karen Blixen (pen-name Isak Dinesen)

Learning to Feel More Grounded

David, 50, says:

My life has felt a bit like sailing a ship around rocks. In the end there are so many rocks that I feel dizzy from sailing around them all the time. I could have done a great deal more with my life if I had not felt like there were so many restrictions.

For example, I haven't flown since 1977. It was a short trip to Spain and I had one hell of a time over it. Before then, if someone sprang a flight on me and told me it left in half an hour I would struggle with that. But if I had three weeks' warning I would be in a state of collapse by the time the plane took off. The problem is the build-up, and that demonstrates to me that my fear isn't just about flying or being in a confined space. After all, I'm passionate about driving. When I'm in my car, cruising along listening to music, I am at my happiest.

The problem for me is lack of control. An aircraft just happens to be the pinnacle of lack of control for me, and my life has become very difficult because of this. I've become incredibly entrenched in a position where I am constantly having to dodge so many things. My partner often suggests theatre trips, and I come up with all these elaborate excuses, but the truth is that I know I would have real trouble being trapped in a theatre surrounded by people.

The core of my fear is embarrassment. I'm worried I'm going to make a real fool of myself. This is not to say that I can't take on new challenges. I can, if I really push myself. And I get elated by doing something I've feared doing, but afterwards I pay with an enormous come-down. I've expended everything I have.

When I'm panicking about losing control, it's really frightening. My mind often seems to run riot. I get carried along with it and it's difficult for me to put the brakes on. I then get into this terrifying circle of reactions. I start to breathe heavily and soon I'm hyperventilating, which in turn makes my eyes very light-sensitive.

Sometimes I think I'm agoraphobic because I'm not good with masses of people or in a crowd situation where I can't control the situation. I almost feel like I'm having an out-of-body experience where I am so over-sensitive to a situation.

I really want to feel more confident and to not feel so phobic about life.

Pete says:

David mig.   . ne is agoraphobic, but it's not always necessary to put a label on your fears. He might worry that he has developed phobic behaviour, but someone who is phobic tends to have their fear with them all the time, from waking up to going to sleep. It defines who they are. David is not like that. There are times, like when he is in his car, when there is no fear at all. In fact, he feels the complete opposite – he loves to be in his car.

Sometimes it's really important to keep our feet on the ground and focus on ourselves. When David is driving he is aware only of his response to what he is doing. But when he's in situations where he is surrounded by other people his focus is not on himself, it's out there with everyone else. His sense of his own space feels very fragile then, because he is worrying about everyone else's reactions.

This has happened so many times that he *knows* he is going to feel like this. This means he begins to panic long before the situation happens. The debilitating build-up is connected with trying to control and predict an uncontrollable and unpredictable future.

David is clearly a sensitive man who feels responsible for other people. He picks up on everybody else's energy, and when he does this he feels himself disappearing. What he needs to do is learn how to bring his focus back to himself. He needs to find a sense of his own space that he can take with him, regardless of where he is.

There is only one fear we all need – the instinctive, primal fear that is meant to protect us from harm or life-threatening situations. But David's fear is about not knowing how to react. This is when people describe themselves as being out of control.

If you fear losing control it can help to concentrate on feelings of being grounded.

In the long run, men hit only what they aim at. Therefore, they had better aim at something high.

Henry David Thoreau

How to Stay Grounded

I frequently use this type of exercise to help people become more aware of the space around them. When we expand our awareness into the space around us, we can slow down any negative self-thoughts.

Perhaps the best place to do this exercise is outside, in a garden, park or field if possible. But you could just do it in the comfort of your own home if that's easier.

You may want to record this exercise onto a cassette tape, so that you can focus better on the exercise and use it whenever you like.

1. Without closing your eyes, become aware that there is actually space around you. Focus on your breathing and expand your awareness into the space that's in front of you. Imagine seeing yourself from the front. Visualize looking at your own face from some distance away.

2. Now be aware that there is space behind you. Imagine looking at the back of your head from behind, from the back of the room, and further beyond, from the horizon.

3. Be aware that there is space to your left ... and to your right ... and above you ... and beneath you. There is just space, all around.

4. If your mind wanders and starts to talk while you are doing this exercise, get your inner coach to help you relax and focus your attention back on to your awareness of the space around you. You don't have to do this perfectly.

5. Do this exercise for a few minutes, and feel supported by the space around you.

6. The next thing I want you to do is to think of a colour that you would associate with being strong, comfortable and relaxed. Any colour will do. If a colour doesn't come to mind, then start with yellow, a good grounding colour.

7. Focus on your chosen colour. Let your mind travel to the heart of that rich, vivid shade.

8. Now imagine at the top of your back, just below your neck, is a circle the size of your hand. The colour is being pumped through that circle into your body. It's travelling all the way down to your toes ... into your hands ... into your heart ... there is so much of this colour inside your body that it makes you feel wonderful.

9. The colour is now so strong, and you're so full up with it, that it starts moving into the space around you ... in front ... behind ... above ... below ... to the right .... to the left.

10. Go back and try the same technique with other colours. Imagine yourself being filled up with each of these colours in turn.

11. Decide which colour you most prefer, and focus on it. Imagine that colour is shining brightly inside you. Then make it brighter, as if you have a control panel and can heighten the intensity of the hue.

12. Turn it up to a seven or an eight inside, so you're radiating this colour. It's pouring out of you now. You are so full of this wonderful, rich colour and it's so strong it's completely filling the space all around you.

The challenge is to practise this exercise in your daily life, to imagine that you are radiating a powerful colour which helps you in the outside world.

The fear of death is more to be dreaded than death itself.

Publilius Syrus

Living with fear takes a lot of emotional energy, and you'll be a past-master at using your imagination – think of all the times you've imagined every worst-case scenario! Next time you are in a situation where you risk losing control, rather than focusing on everything that can go wrong, focus instead on your breathing and on filling yourself and your space with your grounding colour. You'll find this much easier to call upon if you practise it when you're not feeling afraid or stressed. Just by using this technique in your normal daily life, it will be there as a resource when you're feeling afraid of losing control. Use this exercise to start to take responsibility for what is going on inside your head.

Difficulties Make Us Stronger

A man walking along finds a butterfly cocoon. One day, a small opening appears in the cocoon. The man sits and watches as the butterfly struggles for several hours to force its body through the little hole. Then it seems to stop making any progress. It appears as if it has got as far as it can, and can go no further. The man decides to help the butterfly. He gets a pair of scissors and snips off the remaining bit of the cocoon. The butterfly emerges easily, but it has a swollen body and small, shrivelled wings. The man continues to watch, because he expects that, at any moment, the wings will enlarge and expand. Nothing happens. The butterfly spends the rest of its life crawling around with a swollen body and shrivelled wings. It never flies.

What the man in his kindness and haste did not understand was that the restricting cocoon and the struggle required for the butterfly to get through the tiny opening was nature's way of forcing fluid from its body into its wings so it would be ready for flight once it achieved freedom from the cocoon.

To fear love is to fear life.

Bertrand Russell

Sometimes struggle is exactly what we need in our lives.
Edward, 39, says:

I absolutely refuse to go up to high places. When I do, I struggle with the unpleasant feelings this creates. Recently I went to a party on the 5th floor of a block of flats. I had to walk along a narrow passageway with metal railings on one side and a sheer drop beyond. My instinct was to draw back and not to walk along the path, but because of the party, I had to do it. I told myself I was being foolish, aware that if instead of railings there had been a wall I would have had no problems in walking along the same passageway. The only way I could cope was to fix my eyes on the door, but I had a frightening sensation that somehow I was going to be pulled off the safety of the path and over the railings. It made no logical sense, but that was my fear.

On holiday last year in the Blue Mountains of Australia I saw a man-made platform overhanging a cliff. Later I could not physically bring myself to step on to the platform. Unable to cross the divide between what was natural and what was man-made, I experienced a sensation of weightlessness, and had an absolute terror that despite my weight I was somehow going to be swept over the edge and drop, presumably to my death. I felt disembodied and dizzy. There didn't seem to be enough gravity holding me down.

Running alongside this was an anger at myself for not being able to overcome these feelings and step onto the platform like everyone else. A civil war was going on inside me. On one side, my brain was using logic to try and propel me forward to stand on the platform and look over the edge, because I wanted to enjoy the view. On the other hand was a non-rational sensation coming from my body that this was bloody dangerous, and that somehow I would meet my end. I felt weak, powerless and weightless. The unconscious part of me just wanted to run away, to step back and keep stepping back to get as far from the edge as I could.

It wasn't that I feared death. I feared being propelled over the edge and being out of control. I felt a bit unhinged that some unconscious force in my body had taken me over. Despite my brain rushing to rationalize the whole thing, my body just refused to cooperate. Feelings of impending doom crept in, a sense that if I did overcome my fear I would be tempting fate.

I then felt ashamed for not overcoming my fear. Physically and emotionally I felt weak for not being man enough. But the more I stepped away from the edge, retreating from the fear, the more I came back into myself and felt more fully present and in control.

I used to go rock-climbing, but I've noticed that my fear of heights has increased in the past 10–15 years. I last went climbing seven years ago; now it has no appeal. Since I stopped rock-climbing I've taken up scuba-diving, but even underwater the same feeling sometimes hits me. I can't wait to get down to the bottom where I feel more secure.

Fifteen years ago I was involved in a motorcycle accident which put me in a wheelchair for a time and led to subsequent operations. This left me feeling weak and vulnerable.

It's as if being connected to the ground by my feet isn't enough when I'm high up. I feel insignificant, as if I could just be swept away, proving my insignificance. I don't imagine being dashed on the rocks below, instead the focus of the fear is on being brushed away or removed by some force bigger then myself.

I want to feel more grounded and less vulnerable. I want to be able to do what other people do.

Pete says:

This is not a fear of heights, it's a fear of falling which, in turn, is a fear of being out of control. Edward's accident has taught him how important it is to keep both feet on the ground, literally 'to be grounded'. The experience of travelling at high speed in his motorcycle accident has taught him to ensure that he stops history repeating itself. His fear exists to keep him out of a wheelchair. When viewed like this, you can see that this is actually quite an effective and protective form of behaviour.

However, it also has its debilitating side.

If you are scared of heights it can be very helpful to work with colour, as above.

Using your breath is another very effective way of helping you deal with fears to do with losing control. The tendency is to hold your breath at times when we are afraid, which increases the adrenaline in your body and only makes you feel more anxious.

I want you to try something called circular breathing. We'll look at breathing in more detail later, but this is a useful introduction.

Circular Breathing

1.	Close your mouth and take a deep, slow breath through your nose. Enjoy the sensation of this cooling, grounding air.
2.	Open your mouth slightly and let the air filter out naturally, in preparation for the next nasal inhalation.
3.	Close your mouth again and relish breathing in through your nose. Experience the sensation of feeding yourself with air.

Whenever you feel vulnerable or frightened use this technique, remembering that the air you breathe can ground you and relax you.

Fears triggered by something that has happened to us in the past are a *conditioned response* – uncomfortable emotions are set off by something we come across in daily life that reminds us of what has happened before.

The key is to stop concentrating on the feelings, and instead concentrate on the present moment. It is a funny, frightening world and we all pick up fears and worries from things that happened to us in the past. If you are being controlled by these experiences, recognize that you are playing a broken record and give yourself permission to record a better one, using the colour visualization technique above. Record and play this, your new record, anytime you want.

Deflating the Boom

Edward can't change the fact that his accident happened, but he can change the way he thinks about it. I call this 'deflating the boom'. If you've been conditioned into fear after an accident, remember that, although it was shocking and traumatic, you survived and came out the other side.

When you are feeling fear of some project or idea or dream, ask yourself, What am I still curious enough about to override my fear? Follow your curiosity like a delicious scent leading you to a

kitchen. Let your curiosity peel back the dry, bitter skin of drudgery to find the sweet fruit of fun at the core. Focus on what you love rather than fixating on the feelings of discomfort that sometimes accompany desire.

Carol Lloyd

One of the things I do in helping people is to get them to run unpleasant experiences backwards, as if they were watching it happening and seeing themselves in the experience. Running it backwards from the point where you knew you had survived, eventually means it gets so jumbled it won't play anymore. This is a valuable technique that will help you regain control over your fear.

Another technique is to envision the experience with you wearing a silly hat or a clown costume. Go back and watch the accident again in your mind's eye, but this time imagine it's a cartoon. You could have Tom and Jerry in there, you could make it bizarre, you could add silly music. However bizarre this seems, believe me, it works. While you are entertaining these images, your brain is working with its memory trace of the accident and starting to encode it in such a way that it begins to lose its power over you.

All the time, feel the supportive presence of your inner coach. Reassure yourself, be gentle on yourself. Tell yourself that fears are perfectly natural, but that you can get control over them.

Keep playing with these visualizations whenever you have a spare moment.

Flexing Your Mental Muscle

When you feel you can draw on these images easily, you are ready to begin to expose yourself to real-life situations that have, in the past, made you feel fearful or anxious. If you are afraid of heights, try taking a lift while imagining that you are a giant who can step down to earth at any moment. When you go on an escalator or up a flight of stairs, remember that your feet are like heavy tree roots grounding you to the steps.

Above all, allow yourself to relish the simplicity of change. Many people refuse to accept that change can be so easy. But it is.

The Fear of Not Being Good Enough

Without leaps of imagination, or dreaming, we lose the excitement of possibilities. Dreaming, after all, is a form of planning.

Gloria Steinem

Michael, 39, says:

People have congratulated me on certain achievements in the past, such as creating a company out of nothing, which to me didn't feel like an achievement. Instead I felt as if I should have been more successful.

If I've tried to raise funding for a project and I fail, I don't just feel sad about that, instead I question my whole worth and my ability to achieve anything.

I'm deeply afraid of not realizing my potential, of getting to the end of my life not having connected to my passion. I don't seek external approval, I seek my *own* approval and I'm a hard task master. I have a sense, rather than a knowledge, that I'm capable of great things, but I don't know what they are.

I used to be a good sportsman, and I had no doubts about my ability, but then an accident robbed me of my ability. Since then I've never found anything that offers that feeling of being able to achieve.

I try to project ahead to living in a different way, hoping that this will make me feel better, but I can't see myself in a situation where I'm not anxious about my life's meaning.

I fear that I will never be content. I am terrified that there is no place for me – partly because of the way the world works, and partly because I don't know what I should be doing with my life and I fear I won't find out in time.

The fear starts merely as a thought, then it becomes a facial expression as I realize I am frowning. Soon I'm physically agitated and start fidgeting.

Then a feeling of shame creeps in as I tell myself I haven't achieved because I'm lazy and haven't been properly motivated. The message here is: I didn't do enough, therefore it didn't work.

So now I've got guilt and shame swirling around in a vicious circle. Rationally, I know this is not constructive, but it makes it more difficult to break out from these negative feelings.

Sometimes the feeling progresses on to more physically extreme symptoms. These are rare but very intense and unpleasant. As I become more angry with myself, I get shortness of breath and sudden violent twitches. The anger seems to be coming from my body and is directed at my mind. I'm filled with strong feeling that I should be doing more, should be more productive, that I am capable of more greatness than my life currently offers. It's terribly frustrating.

At this point I can actually start to feel light-headed. There's a tingling sensation in my fingers and around my mouth as I begin to hyperventilate. I wrestle with this feeling, using all the well-known strategies for feeling faint. I put my head between my knees, I try and breathe calmly. Superficially, it does work and I get it under control. But the moment it's under control I start to feel quite numb. Some part of my brain is closing down in order to stop myself giving myself a hard time again.

A wise man once suggested I try and stay with that feeling in order to experience why I was having it, but I find it easier to pursue an activity which avoids it, makes me feel good about myself and offers pleasurable feelings. So it's then I'll go off and do something that makes me feel good, something physical that gives me a sensation I can relate to again – sex, food, alcohol or cigarettes.

This is a process of denial and it doesn't help me much. Yes, I can manage the physical symptoms and get myself under control, but then I switch off and deny the state of mind that produced the symptoms in the first place.

The fear creates a knot in my stomach. I feel very anxious and panicked. I look at my life right now and I don't like it. I look at what my life means and I don't find an answer.

I want to feel committed to what I'm doing, to feel passionate about my life. I want to be free from anxiety, to feel sure about what I'm doing because it feels right to be doing it, regardless of what anyone else might think.

I know I have energy, power and potential, but I feel like I can't access them and I fear that I never will.

I'm waiting for an intuition about what I should be doing. I'm full of fear because what will happen to me if it doesn't arrive? What if I sit waiting for my life to unfold for ever?

Thinking like this casts me back into anxiety. My brain rushes to rationalize and make sense of everything. I have to try very hard to quiet my mind.

I want to be able to see what I should be doing. I want to access what's in my soul. I believe in the idea of a calling, and I'm waiting for that call. My fear is that it will never come.

Pete says:

Michael has a fear of not being good enough. But not good enough according to whom? It definitely didn't start with him. So where did this fear come from?

As we grow up we learn to think about the future. Then, through a process of copying, mimicking and absorbing messages from the people around us, we can learn to impose a set of values and ideals that can cause us to struggle.

Michael has probably grown up under a strong influence from his father and perhaps the church. The strong sense of 'should' and 'shouldn't' that defines him is a traditionally male energy, and it can be very destructive.

Michael is paralysed by a sense that he's always got to strive for success and never rest on his laurels. It's the classic work ethic, a set of values that has manifested in all areas of his life, and it's not healthy. He is a product of that belief system, and it is where his problems stem from.

Michael has developed a huge mental comfort zone around his fear of not being good enough. Intuitively I can tell that he would be a difficult case to work with. The fact that he can describe in such detail how he feels means that he has become extremely good at this behaviour. It would be a very difficult step for him to say 'Yes, I'm good at this, I've practised this, but I want to be different.' It would be like leaving behind a huge investment. People often say 'this is the person I am'. Actually, this is the person you are *choosing* to be, at this moment.

The idea of 'staying with a feeling you are experiencing' is used in some self-help approaches. But hang on a second – if you already feel like this for so much of the time, perhaps you've felt like this enough already. If you have experienced a feeling so often that you can describe the symptoms with great accuracy, you have become an expert on what makes you feel bad. You need to change your focus.

If you've spent a long time practising being hard on yourself and sabotaging your happiness, you can really benefit from developing a gentle inner coach. Try the following exercise to find out what sort of inner coach you are currently using.

The principle is competing against yourself. It's about self-improvement, about being better than you were the day before.

Steve Young

Internal Log Book

Keep a daily log by writing down some of the things you talk to yourself about. This is a job and a half, because it's estimated that we have on average 50,000 thoughts every day – but make a start at getting some of it down. The key here is to notice how you talk to yourself. The quality of your life comes down to how you communicate internally. Most people communicate with themselves in a very negative way, constantly criticizing, being worried and being frightened. Would you call up a good friend and talk to them the way you currently talk to yourself? Chances are, you just wouldn't do it. So why do it to yourself? If you wanted to help and motivate your friend to be happy, chances are you'd be kind and respectful. This is a good way to treat yourself.

The most important thing is to see every day as a blank page. You are not here to criticize what you are doing, you are just observing your thoughts.

So many of my clients who try this exercise are shocked when they see in black and white just how negative and repetitive so many of their thoughts are. Once written down, they see patterns of thinking that are boring, out of date and unproductive. This often shakes them into thinking new thoughts, doing things differently and being more positive.

Many spiritual teachers, such as Jesus and Buddha, suggested that you should do unto others as you do unto yourself. If people really did do that, there would be a lot of people out there who wouldn't have any friends. Their friends simply wouldn't put up with the abuse and criticism that they normally give themselves. Would you talk to or treat your best friend the way you treat yourself? So why are you so hard on yourself? You need to stop harming yourself in this way.

I recently helped a woman called Angela. She had been brought up by extremely strict parents and had very little confidence in herself. She believed that if she were successful she would be rejected by people close to her, and she poured all her energy into keeping everyone else happy, neglecting herself. Finally, through our work together Angela realized she was allowed to be nice to herself. This simple instruction has changed her life.

Remember some of the greatest moments in your life and write down five of them. What were you doing? How did you feel? A sentence for each will be sufficient.

Only those who dare to fail greatly can ever achieve greatly.

Robert F. Kennedy

Now look at what you have written. Often, memories stay with us because they happen when we are truly in the moment. There was probably nothing over-analytical going on in your head as you beheld a beautiful sunset, held a newborn baby, or told your partner you felt love for them. Instead, you were suffused with a sense of 'Wow, isn't this amazing?' You weren't thinking about the past or the future, you were just present.

One of the greatest gifts that Michael, Angela and other people who are hard on themselves could give themselves is to be present.

If you are always hectoring yourself or worrying about the future, set yourself a simple task for a day: to enjoy everything you do regardless of the outcome. This is difficult for most people because so many of our values and work ethics follow the 'no pain, no gain' mind set. If you are always striving for success, it can be difficult to do something for the enjoyment of doing them.

I once worked with a top tennis player who put so much pressure on himself that he negatively affected his performance. He explained that in a pressure situation, during the time it took him to throw the ball up in the air and hit it he could remember every single time he'd played his opponent in a similar shot, and replayed it inside his head.

As I'm sure you're aware by now, to be really effective at something you need to be focused on it: Focused on what you are *doing*, not on what's happened in the past, not what possible future might result. This is the problem this tennis player faced. He was someone who thought too much, so much so that it actually disrupted the focus of his performance. Not surprisingly, he didn't win as often as he should have done. If you are an athlete and you focus on something other than the move you are making, you're in trouble.

One of the first sports ever invented was called Zen Archery. It involved riding a horse while holding a bow and arrow. But the sport wasn't about how close to the target you got, rather it was about a state of mind, training yourself not to let go of the bow until your mind was completely clear. Having a clear mind was the purpose of the sport, where the arrow went was secondary. The nature of doing well at sport is not to think. Yogi Berra, one of the most famous baseball coaches of all time, said: 'You cannot hit the ball and think at the same time.' And by the same token, to be effective in life we need to just enjoy what we're doing. Just do it, rather than thinking about it all the time. This is Michael's issue.

It will be a big step for Michael not to be so hard on himself and to work on not being so goal-orientated. He needs to break it all the way down into its simplest form. What is the meaning of life? To try and focus on and enjoy what you do, moment by moment. Finding something you enjoy doing is the first step here.

Michael says he likes to smoke and drink. These can be destructive habits – you drink to get out of your head if you don't like what's in there – but it's understandable why his mind wants to distract him from the negative programmes he's running. Michael used to enjoy sport. He could find another healthy activity, such as golf. To play golf well you have to leave all your problems behind and become totally focused on what you are doing.

We tell ourselves so many lies and half-truths ...We listen and are duly impressed by these inner voices that turn into unseen judges that nag at us. We give each of these judges a seat of honor in our minds, all the while hating their guts and their never-ending supply of judgements ...We give the judges permission to accompany us on each journey of life, never daring to realize that we can park them, at least momentarily.

Eloise Ristad

Give yourself the gift of seeing every day as a blank page or a new birth. You have the ability to transcend everything. See how much of one day you can spend enjoying what you're doing. Many of us over-complicate our lives. Try thinking less and doing more. Try keeping it simple.

Seeing Through Fear

The Past Is Over – Why Are You Still Focusing On It?

I have not ceased being fearful, but I have ceased to let fear control me. I have accepted fear as a part of life – specifically the fear of change, the fear of the unknown; and I have gone ahead despite the pounding in my heart that says: turn back, turn back, you'll die if you venture too far.

Erica Jong

How many times have you said you are going to do something, and not done it? 'I keep meaning to exercise, but I just haven't got around to it,' or 'I was going to lose weight, but I've still not done it.' Well, that's OK. You can beat yourself up about what you *haven't* done, accept that you don't *want* to do those things, or *change your life today if you really want to.*

Life starts *now*. The temptation, however, is to lean back on your past as some kind of prop, or to hold on to your fear as some sort of a security blanket. Allowing yourself to accept that the past is over has the power to wash a huge amount of aggravation out of your system. 'I look on my life as being a great deal to do with the past, and that makes me feel trapped,' one client told me.

If the past makes you feel bad, change your focus.

Tearing Up the Past

So, where do you think your past is? If you had to point to your past, where would it be? In front of you, behind you, below you, above you, to the left, or to the right?

1. Point towards the direction where the past lies for you. Now, allow your mind to travel in that direction, way out into the distance, running right back beyond everything that has happened to you in your life. Push your thoughts a long, long way back and imagine that path stretching for mile upon mile upon mile.

2. Now, imagine that you could stick down some special tape. This tape only sticks to memories and experiences that you don't want to think about, ever again. Press it down over all the bad bits, stretching right into the distance.

3. Now imagine ripping it up – shwooooosh – and it's tearing up every negative experience and memory that you've ever had. All the bad bits cling to the tape.

4. Imagine screwing the tape into a ball and throwing the tape with superhuman strength far into the distance where it explodes into a million, zillion pieces.

A builder friend of mine had just finished a rough first day on the job: a flat tyre made him lose an hour of work, his electric saw broke, and then when it was time to go home his ancient van refused to start. While I drove him home he sat in stony silence. On arriving at his house, he invited me in. As we walked towards the front door he paused briefly at a small tree growing nearby and briefly touched the tips of the branches with both hands.

After opening the door, he underwent an amazing transformation. His face was wreathed in smiles and he hugged his two small children and gave his wife a kiss.

Afterwards, he walked me to my car. We passed the tree and my curiosity got the better of me. I asked him about what I had seen him do earlier. 'Oh, that's my trouble tree,' he replied. 'I know I can't help having troubles on the job, but one thing is certain, my troubles don't belong in the house with my wife and children. So I just hang them up on the tree every night when I come home. Then, in the morning, I pick them up again. But the funny thing is that most mornings I've forgotten what I put there in the first place. It's as if by leaving them behind they begin to sort themselves out.'

When I run workshops I tell the trouble-tree story, because it's such a wonderful piece of imagery. I encourage you now to use it to put your problems to one side, while you focus on enjoying your life. This isn't about avoiding your problems. The process of living without them for a while actually puts them into perspective, making them easier to face, so you soon feel less ruled by them.

The past is important because it is where you come from, but if you feel that your past is actually holding you back, cut out a picture of a tree from a magazine and stick it somewhere where you can see it, as a reminder to focus on the present. If you feel overwhelmed by the past, just touch the picture of the tree to leave your past behind.

Grounding Yourself

I've never been afraid to admit when I've made a mistake. It nearly drives me nuts sometimes, making mistakes. I keep telling myself I should be perfect, but that isn't what we're here for. Perfection isn't an option for us; perfection is death... We're here to learn and change, and that means making mistakes.

Greg Bear

Trees are much older than you. They are grounded and rooted. If you feel overwhelmed by the past, your fears and your worries, make time to go to a park or a woodland and empty your troubles into the nearest tree.

Stand with your back to a tree and just breathe deeply, letting your cares evaporate. Consider how long this tree has been standing there, how it will be standing there long after your problems have vanished, long after you have gone.

You might feel self-conscious or wonder how this will help, but give it a go. Use your imagination. 'The man with no imagination has no wings,' as Mohammed Ali once said.

Sometimes imagination is more important than knowledge. Doing something you wouldn't normally do can often open up a world of unforeseen possibilities and opportunities.

The Importance of Forgiveness

Sometimes we can't move forward, and lose our fears, because we are holding on to too many negative emotions from the past. In Buddhism there is an acceptance that carrying bad feelings around is like holding on to a hot coal in your hand. It hurts. Buddhists don't deny the existence of negative emotions such as fear, worry, stress, anger and guilt, but they champion the benefit of letting go of these uncomfortable feelings.

This can be challenging if these negative emotions are directed at people who have let you down and towards whom you feel angry. Often we want to direct blame and anger at people like our parents, lovers, peers and friends. But if we think like this we are completely overlooking the power of forgiveness.

Forgiveness is a gift we give *ourselves*. If you forgive someone who has done wrong by you, you can stop them having any power over you. If on the other hand you allow your anger to fester, you are allowing that person to continue to control your life. If any of your fears have come about because of something that someone else did to you, you might find that forgiving them helps your fear begin to go away. Give yourself permission to get on with your life.

But what about forgiving yourself? Some of your fears might have come about because you've been too hard on yourself, or feel you're not good enough. This is as good a time as any to get your inner coach to help you through by forgiving yourself for the past, and helping you be more positive in the future. People say 'I'll start tomorrow,' but there is no tomorrow. There is only today. If you're serious about forgiving yourself, do it right here, right now.

The Only Thing You Can Control Is Your Own Attitude

For me, all I can do is spit in the eye of my fears by living each day with as much passion and commitment as possible to what truly counts, such as love and justice. To give into the fear and hopelessness would be to declare defeat, something I am not ready to do while there is still the will to struggle.

Lawrence Paradis

A colleague and I once worked together with a famous British sporting champion who was really struggling to improve his performance. It became apparent to both of us that this person was terrified of losing control.

Now, one reason I'm so passionate and enthusiastic about helping people is that many times the results and benefits are immediate. One time on live television I worked with a woman who was genuinely phobic about spiders. At the beginning of the programme she was terrified even of a tiny money spider in a box in the same room as her. By the end of the programme, this same woman was able to stroke a tarantula. Talk about a result!

So, as you can expect, when I started working with this top sporting champion I was expecting great things. I was in for a shock. I was trying to help him with all the enthusiasm and passion I have, but he appeared disinterested, as if there was a brick wall between us. Everything I said hit the brick wall.

I could see that his biggest fear was of losing control. He was completely resistant to change. The harder I tried, the more resistant he became, until I noticed that my colleague was signalling me to stop. I realized that this athlete was determined to hold on to the way he performs, even though he's got as far as he can using that approach. But there is no point helping someone who doesn't want to be helped.

No one knows everything. As I've said before, science understands only about 5 per cent of how our bodies and brains work. I desperately tried to get this athlete to be open to change, but as the old saying goes, 'You can lead a horse to water but you can't make him drink.'

The problem with nursing an overpowering desire to be in control, as this man did, is that no one can control everything. Where do you draw the line? You can't control the world. You can't stop the wind from blowing in a tree. Your attitude is the only thing that you can control. And change is the only constant of which you can be sure.

Remember earlier on I suggested you practise doing things differently, such as sleeping on the other side of the bed or going to work by a different route? Just remember the importance of being open to change. It's only through changing the way you think and behave that you can make a difference, and get rid of your fear for ever.

I was once contacted by a severely agoraphobic woman who hadn't been outside for three years. She wanted me to visit her and offer assistance. I explained that I couldn't do that, she would have to come and visit me. She was very disturbed by this and said she would think about it. I wasn't hopeful. A few minutes later she phoned back and suggested meeting me in a hotel about a mile from her home. I agreed to the compromise because I could tell that stepping outside was a huge undertaking for her. It showed me that she was ready and committed to change.

When I asked her to explain her fear, she said: 'Whenever I think about going outside I immediately here the music from *The Omen* getting louder and louder. I won't go near the front door. I'm convinced it's about to snap open with a powerful gust of wind and that it will be pitch black outside. I find myself replaying this disturbing fantasy that if I walk outside a van will come to a sudden halt in front of me. The windscreen would shatter and I would be showered with blood.' It's a pretty graphic story, but this woman was not suffering any mental illness. Instead her imagination had become very skilful at having these obsessive thoughts. If you thought like she did, would *you* go outside? Of course not, and neither would I.

Remember, your brain doesn't know the difference between a real experience and one you've made up. What we call memory is nothing more than a recording in the brain, distorted by our unique perception. The inaccuracies, distortions and discrepancies of eyewitness reports is well known. People can swear blind to the veracity of their statement, and they are indeed being true to their own memory, it's just that their memory has been wrongly recorded. The brain records information precisely as it receives it. If what is received is distorted, it is recorded the same way. When it is replayed, the distortion remains.

As you grow older, you'll find the only things you regret are the things you didn't do.

Zachary Scott

We rely on our own perceptions, even when our brain has been affected by alcohol, drugs or intense emotions. Yet the cheapest video camera is far more accurate than our memory.

However, the fact you can fool your brain is a wonderful gift in overcoming your fears. It means that you can easily persuade it to accept a more constructive version of reality.

The Power of Your Imagination

Human beings have a tremendous capacity to see things working, to imagine possibilities, and even to dream things into existence. Learning to use your imagination in a different and empowering way can help you conquer your fear for good.

Using your imagination in this way is known as visualization. Sometimes people think that this is a difficult process, but we think in pictures all the time. What did you have for dinner last night? Where did you spend your last holiday? Who is your best friend? What colour is your front door? In order to see these things, you automatically make a picture of them. Visualization is not a technique; you already do it every day. It is one way human beings process information about their world. Your potential for mastery over your life lies in how you choose to employ this in-built skill.

If you are used to feeling fearful or anxious, you are already very proficient at using your imagination. Visualization is all about using your imagination to empower rather than scare yourself. To visualize effectively, all you need to do is start focusing on pictures rather than words. If you know you want to do something or change something in your life, one of the most effective ways is to visualize it.

In 1992, Sally Gunnell won a Gold Medal at the Barcelona Olympics in the 400 metres hurdles, and became one of only five women to have won gold for Britain. In 1993, she broke the world record and won the World Championships in Seville.

How did she do this? Sally, like many other athletes, struggled throughout her career with injuries. She was even told by a very well-known coach that she was the wrong colour for her event, and the wrong height. But she persevered. In 1991 she was approached by another famous athlete, David Hemery, a former middle-distance runner. He asked if she had ever thought about her races before they happened. Sally said that sometimes the night before a race she would stop and run through it in her head and imagine herself winning.

David explained to her that this wasn't good enough. If she wanted to win a gold medal in Barcelona and become an Olympic champion, she would benefit from spending time visualizing and imagining herself winning, over and over again.

So Sally decided to give it a go. She would imagine going into a stadium with about 85,000 people watching her, plus a couple of billion people watching on television. She imagined going behind the line, feeling the anticipation of the crowd, feeling the adrenaline rushing through her body, and then she would run the race in her head, seeing it in incredible colour and sound. Sometimes she would win the race, and sometimes she wouldn't. When she didn't win the race in her head, she would run it over and over in her mind until she just kept winning.

When she won in 1992, she knew it wasn't just the hard work and dedication to the physical element of her sport, but also because of the right attitude and using the power of her imagination to see herself winning.

She became such an expert at this that in 1993 when she crossed the line in the World Championships, she didn't realize at first that she had won. The power of spending time focusing on what she'd wanted to happen was at work here. And not only had she won, she'd also broken the world record.

The best inspiration is not to outdo others, but to outdo ourselves.

Anonymous

A woman who was frightened to drive on the motorway came to see me. She said that she imagined her car was shrinking and shrinking, while all the other cars were getting bigger and bigger, and that the slightest movement would make her car veer across the road. Another woman was frightened of going outside – she would imagine being attacked. For both these people, the prospect of confronting their fear stopped them from partaking fully in life. Their brains were trying to help them by creating an image of the thing they fear that was so danger-ous and upsetting that, understandably, they would do anything to avoid the fearful situation.

The things we think about, and what we imagine, have a profound effect on how we feel. Thinking about or imagining yourself free from fear gives your brain the option of making this happen for real.

If you want to give up a fearful habit, you need to be able to see yourself how you want to be, free from the fear that is holding you back. You need to pretend, to imagine how you would be living your life as a person who is confident to speak in public, or enjoys the feeling of flying, or who isn't bothered by a spider in the bath.

Images of Joy

1. Recall a wonderful holiday. It can be recent, or it can be from your childhood, but it should feel vivid. Remember some of the things you saw on the holiday, some of the things you smelled and tasted. Reflect on how you felt. Imagine you could just step back into the holiday this moment.

2. Make everything bigger and brighter and bolder and clearer. Turn up any sounds. Increase the intensity of the colours until they become even more saturated. Make the memory more real. Notice how you feel from your nose to your toes, your hands to your knees.

3. Close your eyes and bathe in the intensity of the memory you have ignited for a minute.

    Now open your eyes and think about being on an imaginary beach by yourself. You feel wonderful. The coastline stretches to the left and to the right, as far as the eye can see. You can feel the sun warming you, and the warmth of the fine white sand between your toes. A seagull soars, high up in the sky. The turquoise water gently laps the beach. You feel warm and cozy and comfortable. Close your eyes and bask in this image for a minute.

The brain is such an effective tool because it cannot differentiate between real experience and invented experience. While this is precisely why we are prone to irrational fears, it is also our salvation. Overlaying self-limiting behaviours with more positive approaches to life helps us have the life we want.

The more you can use your imagination to help you in this, the more successful you are likely to be in busting your fear. Vividly imagining yourself as this ex-fearful person allows your body to prepare for the end result. Have you ever thought about what makes a great actor? They don't just turn up and start filming while guessing at playing the part. They are given a script, and they use their imagination to become the person they are portraying. Have you ever seen an actor playing a part so effectively that when you see him later being interviewed on television, you can't believe what he is really like? He had so completely occupied the role that you thought this was who he really was.

Take the time to imagine how you'd be if you didn't have your fear.

Ingenuity, plus courage, plus work, equals miracles.

Bob Richards

The Future You

1. Stand up and imagine that you are facing your front door. The door is closed, but behind it lies your future without fear.

2. Grasp the imaginary door handle and pull it towards yourself. The door opens and you can see the back of yourself, in the future, having conquered your fear.

3. Notice what you are wearing, how you are standing.

4. Now the future you is going to turn to the side so you can see yourself in profile.

5. Next, your future you turns to face you. You can see that you look vibrant, amazing, full of life.

6. See the future you in as much detail as you like. Move around so you can get a really good look.

7. Now imagine stepping into the future you. Feel how it is to have conquered your fear.

8. Now do it again. Imagine stepping into the future you again, and intensify those positive feelings.

9. Feel the change in every cell of your body, your organs and your bones.

10. Relish how you feel, as you see through those eyes and hear through those ears, in a life without fear.

11. Once you have finished, take a few deep breaths.

When you are ready, do the exercise again, only this time imagine you've been practising it for years. Practise this exercise every day. Why not go out and pretend to actually be this person?

In one research experiment, three groups of basketball players were prepared for practice. The first group was allowed on the court to practise with a ball. The second group was allowed onto the court, but were instructed to just *imagine* themselves playing there. The third group was left in the changing room to imagine themselves playing. Each group was told to try to get the ball into the basket as many times as possible.

Once each group had had time to 'practise' in the way that they had been instructed, all three groups were allowed onto the court to see which could score the most points.

The first group were not very much improved over their usual scoring record, having been able to practise missing as well as scoring. The second group had improved, but, being on the court, had also imagined themselves missing. It was the third group who got the ball through the net the most often. Away from the court, in the seclusion of a room where their imaginations could travel freely, they had imagined themselves scoring every time.

It's lack of faith that makes people afraid of meeting challenges, and I believed in myself.

Muhammad Ali

Reducing the Size of the Thing You Fear

Fears fall into two different categories: physical fears and abstract fears.

Physical fears are things like being afraid of heights, spiders, flying or social situations.

Abstract fears are things you can't see, such as change, failure, the unknown, the future and losing control.

To test if yours is a physical fear, try and visualize it. You can probably imagine an aeroplane, a spider, a difficult colleague or neighbour, a tall building. Abstract fears are harder to pinpoint visually in this way.

The following exercise can help you to diminish the power over you that physical fears have.

Shrinking Your Fear

1. Create a mental picture of the thing you fear. Now change its dimensions. If you are scared of social situations, imagine that the people you are going to meet are the size of peanuts. If you are scared of flying, imagine looking down on a tiny plane. If you are scared of small spaces, imagine yourself as a teeny, tiny person surrounded by acres of space.

2. Encourage the image to become as ludicrous as possible, and fill it with movement and colour and sound. If you are scared of flying, imagine yourself wearing two plane-shaped roller skates. If you are scared of your boss, imagine him or her as a tiny dot of a person who is shouting to be heard but all you can hear is a distant squeaking. If you are afraid of being in a tall building, imagine yourself playing with cardboard boxes which look like buildings and which you can stack and rearrange at your whim.

    Whatever your fear, diminish it to a point where it is unable to affect you and where you are controlling it. Enjoy feeling strong, confident and having fun.

Think of your imagination as being like a muscle in your body. You can make it stronger, just as you can make any muscle stronger, if you exercise it. One of the similarities between your muscles and your brain is that the more you use them, the more they'll work for you. You wouldn't expect to go to the gym once and suddenly develop bigger muscles; you wouldn't expect to have one driving lesson and be able to drive perfectly afterwards. You work muscles by using them repeatedly. You push the boundaries of comfort again and again until you get the results you want. The same goes for training your brain. Repetitive practice makes perfect practice.

It's not necessarily the amount of time you spend at practice that counts; it's what you put into the practice.

Eric Lindros

I do a lot of work with people who are afraid of confined spaces. After they learn visualization techniques to diminish the hold that their fear has over them, it is remarkable how the things that used to frighten them – like getting into a lift or other small space – become like a stroll in the park. When you change the way you think about your fear and realize that it's just a habit you've got into that can be broken by reprogramming your imagination, it's rather like a switch has been flicked.

The Fear of Revealing Yourself

If a man harbours any sort of fear, it percolates through all his thinking, damages his personality, makes him landlord to a ghost.

Lloyd Cassel Douglas

Clare, 33, says:

I'm standing in front of a group of six strangers at a party, holding a drink in my hand. I'm shuffling my feet, trying to connect myself to the ground, to find a position that feels natural. Suddenly, someone directs a question at me and 12 eyes swivel in my direction. I swallow and try to control the colour rushing to my face. I want this moment to pass as quickly as possible. I get sweaty palms and I can't swallow properly. I can feel an increase in my pulse-rate. I try to relax my face and realize I can't correctly set the muscles around my mouth and eyes. It is very important that I appear confident; now the fear that my fear will be visible adds to my terror. All the while my brain is trying to create and deliver a response that conveys a sense of who I am to the group, while deflecting further enquiry. I'm desperately keen to talk to just one person. The intimacy of that encounter would give me room to breathe, to feel comfortable and relaxed.

I hate the rush of group encounters where everyone is competing to speak and no one is really listening. I just want to opt out and do something else.

When I am faced with talking to a group, I fear being unfavourably judged. This is odd because I'm comfortable with who I am. However, I am aware that I'm not like a lot of other people and have different values and ideals. For example, I'm not cynical and tend to see the best in people. Inevitably I feel frustrated that I don't feel more at ease projecting my individualism to a wider audience. It takes energy to cope as well as I do. Because I find these situations extremely draining, I am very happy to avoid them and I miss nothing about them. I'm always thrilled when social situations are cancelled at the last minute, even those with quite close friends. People always apologize that they are letting you down, but I'm always delighted. I can stay at home and do the things I really want to do.

I'm much happier with just one or two other people. Also, I love reading aloud and acting in plays. In those situations I feel excited, not fearful.

I've learned to mask my feelings of discomfort very well. People who meet me in a group are very surprised later to hear about the high-speed paddling that was going on. Instead, they remark on my serenity.

Although I know my feelings are irrational, that doesn't release me from their grip or their intensity.

My most extreme fear is public speaking, an environment where none of the normal feedback occurs and it's even more difficult to measure a response. If I imagine myself speaking off-the-cuff or even with notes, I imagine drying up, or trying feebly to make a joke. Being able to make people laugh is the most terrifying part. I could talk with intensity with far less difficulty. I've always been glad that I will never have to make a humorous best man's speech at a wedding! At my own wedding I read something I had written myself that was heartfelt, open and true to myself.

I'm obviously aware that in a group or public speaking, there aren't the visual and verbal cues that you get with one or two individuals – nods, facial expressions, etc. The absence of this kind of support makes me feel very exposed, and the encounter feels superficial. I work hard on not caring about the judgement of the rest of the group because I know such fears are pointless.

The irony is that I was teased at school for my voice, but I didn't let it affect me then. Why now as an adult – when I am not subjected to criticism – should I so fear it?

Pete says:

This is a very common fear. When Clare was at school people made fun of her voice, which made her feel there was something wrong with her. Now she is repeating the thoughts and behaviours associated with being teased without even thinking about it. It's an automatic, conditioned response.

Fear of public speaking is a very common fear in the Western world. For many people it is a fear about being exposed and not being good enough, about being judged and found wanting.

Clare is visualizing so beautifully, but unfortunately she is choosing to replay a rather scary movie. Every time she gets into a social situation in which she is not comfortable, she starts running this programme, so it's no wonder she feels so uncomfortable. With these sorts of intense images, naturally she will want to avoid these situations at all costs. Anyone sensible would react the same way.

It's OK to feel nervous and frightened, but why put yourself through the scary movie if you don't have to? If you do feel nervous or debilitated in social situations, then give yourself permission to stay away. If you'd like to feel more confident, start with smaller goals. Don't go running a race blind. If you do, you can either expect to finish last or to get exhausted.

Clare feels comfortable when she is acting, for two reasons. First, because her focus was on something outside herself. Secondly, because she was not teased at school for her acting skills. Plenty of people are terrified of getting up on stage, but perfectly comfortable at a party. Our current reactions are a map to our past experiences.

Feeling uncomfortable in social situations is a fairly universal fear, because we've all had plenty of opportunity to feel that we don't fit in. Many people in our society are obsessed with conforming, probably because so many people feel that pretending to be something they are not is the only way to be. All sorts of people get teased at school – children who speak well and children who speak badly. Less intelligent children don't fit, but neither do the really clever ones. Clare is trying to be herself.

Often we are surrounded by people who are not really being them-selves. Being around other people who are pretending to be something they're not is often not a particularly nourishing experi-ence. Give yourself permission not to be around people whom you feel uncomfortable with.

Chances are at least a couple of the other people in the group Clare describes were not feeling particularly comfortable either, and may have developed different strategies for masking their fear, typically smoking or drinking. Most of us feel we've got to try to fit in, so we numb ourselves in a socially acceptable way, how-ever destructive this may be.

If you are fearful in social situations, for whatever reason, you need to put your focus of attention somewhere else. It is also important to work out what you actually want. A common sugges-tion from someone who is socially uneasy is to say, 'I don't want to be frightened in social situations.' But that leaves rather a vacuum, in which the focus is still on the fear.

Now let's get you ready to feel more confident. The key here is to get your inner coach working on your side. Your inner coach is going to be with you in your bid to make the whole thing a fun experience.

Most people think that courage is the absence of fear. The absence of fear is not courage; the absence of fear is some kind of brain damage. Courage is the capacity to go ahead in spite of the fear, or in spite of the pain. When you do that, you will find that overcoming that fear will not only make you stronger but will be a big step forward toward maturity.

M. Scott Peck

Rewriting Your Experience

Imagine being in control in a social situation. See yourself standing confidently, observing what's going on, and feeling good. Now write down how you would like to feel.

A single reason why you *can* do something is worth a hundred reasons why you can't. If you can't imagine it clearly, you can't expect it to happen.

If you'd like to feel more confident socially, refuse all party invitations and spend time with close friends. Gradually extend your experiences into small gatherings where most people are known to you. The key is to practise in social situations where you know everyone and feel fairly comfortable. Pretend it's a game, the goal of which is to observe what's going on, rather than being critical of yourself. Listen more, talk less. That's why we've got two ears but only one mouth.

One of the best ways to overcome fear is to focus on your breathing. In this situation, I'd recommend concentrating on exhalation. Breathe out fully, imagining your fear dissipating with every breath. If you feel nervous, take your focus back to your breathing and hear your inner coach saying something constructive such as 'You're fine, this is easy.'

Often the thought of social situations can be worse than the situation itself. If you are about to be involved socially, try making a helpful mental video. Instead of the scary movie that's already playing at the cinema in your mind, you've got to film a better one.

This is a good time to get a pen and paper and pretend you are writing a screenplay. You are the director, the writer and the producer. You can use the following exercise to help you see, hear and feel what it would be like to be yourself, free from fear.

It's a waste of this life not to live this life. What's next is anybody's guess.

Malcolm Forbes

Making a Better Movie

1. Create a detailed setting for the party. See yourself standing or sitting and feeling comfortable and confident.
2. Imagine the picture moving closer and closer towards you, until you fill the screen.
3. Inject that image of yourself with twenty times the confidence.
4. Now boost the confidence up a hundred times.
5. Allow yourself to savour what that feels like. Like an actress or actor, this is the role that you're going to go and play at the party.
6. Focus on how you will feel when the party is over after you've had a wonderful time.
7. Play the new tape in your mind and let your inner coach back it up with positive comments. The thought of everything being okay is like a muscle; for best results keep working on it.

At first you may feel that if you pretend to be confident, you're not being the real you. But you're creating the new you with every new moment – a confident, accepting you – and who's to say that's not the real you, the you you were meant to be?

Finally, remember that your perception of what everyone else is like and what they are thinking is purely that: your own perception, your own creation. You'll find this way of thinking is very liberating.

Don't Give Away Your Fear

A friend of mine has two aunts. One aunt always says: 'Bye, have a great time.' The second aunt always says: 'Bye, be careful.' Every time my friend hears the second aunt saying this, he hesitates for a moment. 'For a fleeting second I find myself thinking "be careful of what?" and I get a little tiny stab of fear as I remember that things might not work out,' he says. These two parting comments create wildly different mental pictures. Both aunts wish their nephew well, but each tells us a lot about expectations and projected fear.

If you are fearful for other people, you're not helping them. People who are afraid of flying often worry if people they love are flying. If we are scared of something, it is only natural for us to feel fearful when our nearest and dearest are in a situation that we personally find difficult.

This sort of thinking is in no way beneficial for either person. Energy follows thought.

If you feel fearful for the people you love, focus your attention instead on a picture of what you want to happen. Make a

picture of them being safe and happy. Imagine them with a protective bubble wrapped around them, wherever they are. This
applies to anything in your life that you want to happen. You
need to make a picture of how you would like things to be.

Nobody grows old by merely living a number of years. People
grow old only by deserting their ideals. Years wrinkle the face,
but to give up enthusiasm wrinkles the soul. Worry, doubt, self-
interest, fear, despair – these are the long, long years that bow
the head and turn the growing spirit back to dust.

Watterson Lowe

6

Embracing Fear

Religion, politics and the media condition us in different ways to be more fearful than we need to be. Information communicated globally can be misleading. 'Man Bites Dog' is a story precisely because it's a rarity. 'Dog Bites Man' happens all the time, and therefore doesn't make the headlines. When we are fed a constant diet of murder and mayhem, if we read countless stories about abduction and abuse, it is easy to believe that these terrors are a clear and present danger in our daily lives. We may think twice about walking outside alone, or letting our children play in the park.

Your only limitations are those you set up in your mind, or permit others to set up for you.

Og Mandino

We are inculcated in the belief that planes are constantly falling out of the sky, because once or twice a year there is an accident or a near-miss on all the front pages. Plane crashes are unusual. That's why we hear about them. Worldwide, thousands of people die on the roads every day. Fewer than a thousand are killed in the air every year. We should actually be much, much more afraid of cars than of planes. But we can only be afraid of what we *perceive* to be a threat.

Why Do We Entertain Ourselves with Fear?

This book aims to empower you by demonstrating that most forms of fear are not only unnecessary but actually do not exist, other than in your own imagination. The mind is so powerful, it can create fear where none exists. When you feel fearful of something it *feels* completely real – to one part of your mind.

A perfect illustration of this is what is known as *recreational fear*. Like a kitten honing its hunting skills by chasing shadows and inanimate scraps of paper, adult humans love to terrify themselves, producing adrenaline responses to symbolically terrifying stimuli, as this man, who relishes horror movies and roller-coaster rides, says:

I adore the sensations of fear that these things raise in me. I don't often experience these powerful feelings in daily life, and they are interesting to me because they reveal unfamiliar dimensions of my mind and imagination. I wish I could be young again to watch horror films like I used to, when they would really scare me in a delightfully horrific sense. I knew they weren't real, but they had the power to really freak me out. Now I'm older I know they are more transparent, so getting those juices and chemicals of being out-of-control flowing, is much more difficult. But it does happen. When you are watching a horror movie, when some horrific act is about to occur your imagination projects your body into the scene. You know you're not there, but it's a safe place to experience the terror. As for a roller-coaster, that's all about throwing yourself off a building with a seat belt on.

The rational part of you stays under control – you know it's just a theme park or film – but other parts of you are fooled: your heart rate increases, your throat constricts and your palms may sweat. I derive a certain sense of sick pleasure from these feelings. They are unpleasant, but being able to feel and express them is a delight. It's always followed by a power rush, knowing you've survived.

Often our fearful responses are in direct opposition to the actual threat we feel. When you watch a horror movie, the likelihood that there is a man in a mask outside your house is virtually nil – it's a completely safe experience. A roller-coaster ride is also in reality. But if you are facing an encounter with a hostile neighbour there is every likelihood that you will exchange stormy words – the experience may not be life-threatening, but it differs from recreational fear in that it is 100 per cent real.

What this shows us is that fear can be pleasurable, exciting and exhilarating – when you are able to control your response to it. A roller-coaster that didn't get you screaming would be a very dull experience. These people have learned to use fear. They choose to get on the roller coaster because they are giving themselves permission to enjoy being frightened. Mastering and overcoming their chosen terror gives them a fabulous high.

Obstacles are like wild animals. They are cowards but they will bluff you if they can. If they see you are afraid of them... they are liable to spring upon you; but ... if you look them squarely in the eye, they will slink out of sight.

Orison Swett Marden

What We Learned from *Jaws*

The 70s film *Jaws* changed the way we viewed the world. Before the film was made sharks were probably not uppermost in most people's list of fears, but today, those of us who have seen it may well find it virtually impossible to enter the sea for a swim without running a little movie called *What If a Shark Bit My Leg* in our heads. *Jaws* and its sequels effectively demonized sharks. They were no longer just large fish; instead they became a symbol of all that scares us: Sinister malevolence, invisibility, unpredictability, terrifying violence and powerlessness. We can only be attacked by a shark when we are in the sea, an environment that makes many of us feel vulnerable and where we have no tools with which to fight back. This increases the power and resonance of this particular fear.

Like the best horror movies, there was actually very little violence in the *Jaws* films. Instead, what we were offered was menace, suspense and threat – just the sort of situations that play with our fight/flight response. Watching a nature documentary in which a fish or a mammal bloodily kills its prey is fascinating, but it isn't scary. It's not the blood that terrifies us, it's the suspense. Hitchcock was a master of this sort of suspenseful shadow play, serving up scenarios where something dreadful *might* happen at any time.

The Blair Witch Project was similarly successful. This is a film where you don't actually see anything gruesome or bloody, instead it's all down to your imagination. I had to keep reminding myself that there were cameramen there in order to keep a grip on my emotions. Audiences were further engaged by the publicity hype that accompanied the film, which suggested the story might actually be true.

Scary movies work because people *like* to be frightened – in safe, controlled ways. *Jaws* made a generation hide behind the sofa, unable to tear their eyes away. It was so effective that John Williams' famous theme music has become closely identified with feelings of fearful suspense in our culture. The emotional temperature of any encounter can be enhanced by just tunelessly uttering a few of those rapidly increasing 'duh, duh, duh, duh' notes. We all know what it means, and it makes our individual sense of unease easier to bear. We are not the only person who is scared; we all respond in a similar way to the same trigger. Curiously, sharing the experience has the power to make us feel safe.

We change constantly. Just as our cells die and are replenished every few months, new ideas present themselves continuously, opportunities bubble forth – and our magnificent brains, all the while, keep processing millions of bits of information every day. If we're going to recognize and take advantage of the opportunities life affords us and at the same time worry well, we must accept this fundamental rule: To succeed, we must be prepared to fail.

Walter Anderson

Anatomy of a Fearful Encounter

In May 2002, two UK television presenters, Trinny Woodall and Susannah Constantine, were victims of a classic Cote d'Azur robbery. Someone crept into their hotel room and knocked them out with chloroform while they were sleeping. While they were comatose, their possessions were stolen. 'It was a really unpleasant incident and we just want to put it behind us,' said Trinny Woodall with typical British sangfroid. But the desire to 'just get over' such an event is not as easy as we might wish.

A few days after the robbery, writer Lesley Garner wrote an account in London's *Evening Standard* of her own experience, one that closely mirrored the French incident. 'Getting over it isn't so easy, as I found when I woke to the ultimate nightmare: a burglar in my bedroom.'

She continued:

It was four in the morning. My husband was away. The children were tiny and tucked up in their beds, but they were still at the stage of sleepwalking into my room in the middle of the night, so a few nocturnal noises were par for the course. Something woke me up – small, scratchy noises, somewhere beyond the rim of my consciousness. No pad of little feet, no warm body, but still those indefinable rustlings. I opened my eyes and realized that the room – which was L-shaped with the bed in a recess – was illuminated by a dim light. I couldn't see what was happening around the corner. I was profoundly puzzled, but not scared. Whatever was happening was too unprecedented and undefined to have formed into a threat. In fact it was so dreamlike that I closed my eyes again, but it didn't go away. So, without the idea of a burglar

having even formed clearly in my mind, I crept out of the bed and around the corner of the recess and came face to face with a figure, right there in the sanctuary of my bedroom, rifling his way through my shelves.

I still didn't have time to be frightened, because the burglar was terrified first. He let out a yell of horror, like a man who has seen a ghost, and legged it – thank God – through the bedroom door. He ran down the stairs while I, electrified by a massive surge of adrenaline, screamed abuse at him down the stairwell, even as my hands were grabbing the phone and dialling 999.

The police came en masse and very fast. It was while I was watching men and dogs pour through my quiet suburban house that the adrenaline began to subside. Suddenly, I felt shocked and faint and my legs began to shake. Like all survivors, once the first shock was over I realized how lucky I'd been. My family and I seemed to have survived unscathed, losing just a few quid. It took some days to discover the greatest loss of all.

The next night, alone because my husband was still away, I hallucinated that somebody was hiding in the bedroom cupboards. I heard a noise and, heart thudding, I flung myself at the cupboard doors to trap the intruder. Very slowly, as the adrenaline subsided, I realized that there was nobody there. Even after my husband came home, I sat upright at the slightest sound and lay, sleepless, listening to every creak. A sudden noise would set my heart pounding again with an adrenaline surge that prevented further sleep.

For more than a year I woke at the slightest sound and, although I'm over it now, I still love the sense of extra security of sleeping in hotels and other people's houses. The most precious thing burglars steal isn't jewellery. It's peace of mind.

Lesley's experience is a classic example of how our brain works hard to try to protect us. This is why during the year following the break-in, she tormented herself as her brain was trying to prevent her from having another similar experience. This meant she was living, every day, with the fear of what had happened.

The only way to move on is to let go. One of the things I do with people who have had similar experiences is to encourage them to look at the *positive* parts of what happened. Lesley is alive, she survived, and so did her family. She got through it. It's over.

If each of us can be helped by science to live a hundred years, what will it profit us if our hates and fears, our loneliness and our remorse will not permit us to enjoy them?

David Neiswanger

When you've had a frightening experience, you need to take practical meaures to avoid something similar happening in the future – in Lesley's example, shutting downstairs windows when she goes to bed. Beyond that, you need to focus on the here and now, on the moment, as opposed to obsessing about what happened in the past or could happen in the future. Worrying about something means you are investing your focus of attention on it. And remember, as I've said before, we tend to get what we focus on. Even though it might not happen physically, if you keep on thinking about it, it will be happening in your mind all the time, which can be equally terrifying.

What Happens to You When You Are Afraid

Fear is an emotional and physical response to real or perceived danger. It is strong and unpleasant.

When you feel afraid, your brain sends a message to the adrenal glands to release adrenaline, a natural hormone secreted in response to danger. It's your ally and its job is to prepare the body for action – either to run away or to fight.

The process of fear comprises four steps:

1. The Pre-Event Adrenaline Drip: This is a state of fear. It occurs often and is commonly called stress or anxiety. It is intended to put you on alert, mentally and physically. Brain chemicals called neuro-transmitters are released which give you heightened mental focus. You feel tense, nervous and on edge. If this state is prolonged, it can exhaust you and lead to 'burn out'.

2. The Primary Adrenaline Dump: This state is the ultimate survival tool, as your body is prepared for action as a frightening event occurs. Your adrenal glands receive a trigger to dump massive amounts of adrenaline into your system to prepare you for major physical activity. This is a very rapid and intense process; muscles are tightened in preparation for trauma. The heart-rate soars and the breathing rate increases to seize more oxygen. If required, chemicals are released into the bloodstream that give a sudden boost of additional physical strength. Blood is directed away from less critical parts of the body. It means your skin turns white, your vision is focused – leading to tunnel vision – and you temporarily lose a high percentage of your hearing (this is why athletes at major sporting

events can't hear the crowds). People who can channel this stage into productive use excel in intense physical situations such as high danger sports. They can also become addicted to the heightened levels of adrenaline in their body, leading to adrenaline addiction.

3. The Secondary Adrenaline Dump: This is the 'second wind' of endurance. Another big dump of adrenaline gives a secondary rush of energy, heightening the effects described above, and also helps to block pain. This state explains why some people's performance improves as a game or fight goes on, and why footballers try to get hit a few times to 'get into the flow' of the game.

4. The Post-Event Adrenaline Drip: After an encounter, the adrenal glands continue to release small amounts of adrenaline, allowing you to mentally repeat the event and relive the experience. This is intended to help your body readjust to the effects of the stressful situation. When extended over time, however, this leads to physical and mental exhaustion.

Youth is not a time of life; it is a state of mind. People grow old only by deserting their ideals and outgrowing the consciousness of youth. You are as old as your doubt, your fear, your despair. The way to keep young is to keep your faith young. Keep your self-confidence young. Keep your hope young.

Luella F. Phelan

To learn to harness fear, as we will see later, the first step is to recognize that it is *normal*. Insight and knowledge can help you understand what is going on when you are afraid. This is the first stage towards being able to channel the extra energy from the adrenaline for your own purposes, such as meeting dead-lines effectively, winning a physical game, or thinking on your feet under stressful situations.

What Martial Arts Can Teach Us About Fear

Many Westerners trained in some form of martial arts (karate, jujitsu, etc.) fear that if someday they need to defend them-selves or their loved ones in a real situation, they will hesitate or freeze. They are usually right. Most martial artists spend years sharpening their physical skills, but little or no time developing their mental ones. They fall into the trap of thinking that physical technique alone will help them cope in a genuinely violent encounter. Then, when something nasty does happen, they are shocked at their fearful response and the panic they feel. As an attacker gets closer they feel doubt and fear. Their hands shake, their vision narrows, their hearing shuts down, their minds race with negative thoughts. They wonder why their training has let them down.

The reality is that they've neglected to train their brains as well as their bodies, unlike martial artists in the East. To train the mind to resist fear, you must first be able to recognize the differ-ence between the psychological state we label as *fear*, which is accompanied by 'the adrenaline drip', and the quite distinct form of physical fear called 'the adrenaline dump'.

Whether we are martial artists or not, we need to separate our physical responses from our psychological interpretations of them. Doing this can open the door to channelling this wonderful, power-packed state into something that can give you the edge.

Why Fear and Excitement Are the Same Thing

Think again about a roller-coaster. People scream with excitement. Have you ever noticed that fear and excitement often display very similar symptoms, or even wondered why? The answer is simple. They are one and the same. The only difference is our perception of the event.

If we perceive a pleasant outcome, we feel excited. If we perceive an unpleasant one, we feel apprehension. This is why two people doing exactly the same thing can have completely different reactions to it.

Adrenaline can produce many reactions. Everyone feels the effects of adrenaline; there are no exceptions. The only difference is the way we *react* to it. Either we control it, or it controls us.

We need to remember that our reaction to any situation depends not on the situation itself but purely on our individual perception of it. The key to coping with adrenaline is keeping it within manageable levels and not panicking when we feel it, as this can lead to the release of more.

Anxiety, fear that something bad may happen, is at the core of many of our self-defeating responses.

Jeanne Segal, Ph.D.

There are many athletes, especially sprinters, who experience terrible cramp in the heat of competition. Because of the expectations of the crowd, they heap pressure on themselves. As the adrenaline pumps their breathing changes, becoming quicker and more shallow, which robs their muscles of oxygen, making their muscles tighten up. Self-doubt then creeps in. Midway through the race their body, their physical machine, suddenly falls them utterly.

When I work with athletes, I encourage them to try to *get the butterflies flying in formation*. The way to do that is to focus on your breathing. Focus *through* what you are doing, onto the result you want. Don't get caught up on the process of fear itself.

If a situation is challenging, but not threatening, we may enjoy the risk or even feel that we can perform exceptionally well. If we feel we are in danger, we may react with panic or aggression.

I once met a world-champion boxer, and asked him how he would look at someone he was about to fight. He stared at me, hard. Immediately I felt my bowels move – and it wasn't the curry I'd eaten the night before. 'I'm looking at the back of your head,' he said. I asked him why. 'That's where my fist is going. I'm not stopping at the front of your head, I'm going right through you.'

In the same way, sometimes when we have a problem we need to try and see through it to the other side. If you are afraid of flying, for example, you need to focus on what lies right through your fear, on being in another country, having a whale of a time.

Ask yourself the following question: If I had a choice, would I prefer to feel scared or ready for action?

An Adrenaline Diary

I suggest you keep a daily Adrenaline Diary. In your diary, record any incident that has produced adrenaline during the day. Include all those occurrences that created fear, excitement or some other strong emotional response. Make a note of what you were doing, what you were thinking and how you felt.

The diary is a simple inventory of your actions and reactions. The goal is not to eliminate adrenaline from your life, but to understand how you can use it to your advantage.

Remember, we would not have been born with this vital internal chemical if it did not serve a useful purpose. That purpose may be of far greater benefit than the production of a simple fight or flight reaction. All forms of pleasure and joy, including those we seek in blissful experiences, may rely on adrenaline as one of their components.

Be aware, also, that just as some of us ride roller-coasters for fun, we may, even unconsciously, seek out feelings of danger, excitement and fear. There is an addictive quality to the relief we feel when the ride is over and we have overcome our own fears and survived.

Learning to Ride the Roller-Coaster

You may want to go and ride a real roller-coaster, but I'm talking about the roller-coaster that is life. You don't have to throw yourself off a mountain to get a high from your existence.

The great enemy of creativity is fear. When we're fearful, we freeze up ... Creativity has a lot to do with a willingness to take risks. Think about how children play. They run around the playground without thinking about where they're going. They trip, they fall down, and then they get back up again and run some more. They have a wonderful belief: that everything will be all right. They feel capable; they let go; they play... No matter how many facts and figures you have, you can't predict the future. There will always be surprises ...Creativity helps us realize that we don't have to understand everything. We can enjoy something – feel it and use it – without ever fully comprehending it.

Faith Ringgold

Life is full of ups and downs. When you are going up there is real anticipation, a kind of 'Wow, what's going to happen?' Then you go over the top and into a dip, screaming 'Oh my God.' Speed up the visual imagery and you get a sense of the pace of life: anticipation followed by fear followed by achievement followed by anticipation.

You're on this roller-coaster called life, and you have a choice. You can either enjoy it or be terrified by it. Of course, some people choose to stop the ride, rather than really going for it. If this sounds like the past you, or even the present you, bear in mind that you only get one go on the roller-coaster of life.

What *Who Wants To Be a Millionaire?* Teaches Us about Excitement

You can feel your fear muscles working as the blue lights dim and the clock ticks on relentlessly. The contestant has £500,000 on credit and is only one question away from the magic million, but if they answer incorrectly they will walk away with just £32,000. Your palms are sweating. You're on the edge of your seat ... but you're not going to walk away with a penny, whatever the outcome on the television screen in front of you. You've got absolutely no control over the response that is about to spring from the lips of the sweating contestant – and no control over the vicarious fear you are feeling.

Their answer is incorrect. You wring your hands in disbelief, slumping back in your chair as the adrenaline floods out of your system.

We have become so involved in someone else's experience that we can easily fool ourselves into believing that we were the person so close to winning a million pounds.

This is the way that torturers control their victims. They put their victims into a state where they are anticipating a situation, even though it has not actually happened.

We do this to ourselves all the time. We torture ourselves with our fear. We talk ourselves out of doing things because we believe we are afraid. We need to realize that, just like the response we have to a million pounds we are not going to win, our fearful responses are an illusion and a fantasy. They are nothing more than mental projections.

Rename Your Fear

Any kind of intensity generates adrenaline. There are those of us who enjoy this reaction. But for many of us, the presence of adrenaline is uncomfortable. There are some for whom even a mild amount of adrenaline creates a feeling of anxiety. Other people are on a lifelong search for challenge and excitement. The very feelings that other people label 'fear' are for them a delicious sensation which they actively seek out, and might label thrill-seeking, risk-taking, competition, combativeness or passion.

When you feel nervous, give that feeling another label. Imagine you are about to be late for a deadline. You can feel butterflies in your stomach. Stop thinking of that as anxiety or stress, and pick another word. You might choose 'the rush', 'amped up', 'jacked up', 'buzzing', 'ready to go'.

When you are putting demands on yourself, realize that you should *expect* to have butterflies in your stomach. You heart is designed to beat faster to help you cope with pressure situations. Understand that the adrenaline you are feeling has the power to help you perform at your best. You have only chosen to label these feelings as fear.

We are often told that if we feel these sensations it is a sign that we are scared and weak. In reality, we are becoming faster, stronger, pain-resistant and explosive. We *need* adrenaline. Like food, it is necessary to our health and well-being. Without it we would be at greater risk of being hurt.

Changing Your Relationship to the 'Butterflies'

Your orientation to this pumped-up feeling, your interpretation of it, makes it either fear or excitement. So make it excitement by thinking of it in those terms. Welcome the feeling, and use it when you need to ride that roller-coaster, be it public speaking, a meeting with your boss or sorting out an issue with a neighbour.

Every time you think about it you probably get a little adrenaline rush. Use it as a reminder. Even the smallest passing thought probably gives you that rush. So, every time you feel it, use the sensation as a cue to think about what you really want to happen: I want to win, I want to get my point of view across, I want to speak to these people, I want to feel happier. Think of as many positive things as you can about what you want to achieve from the task ahead, and make each adrenaline rush a new infusion of that desire.

One truth about the brain is that it is programmed to believe what you tell it. If you tell it you can, you're right. But if you tell it that you can't, you're also right. What version of reality would you prefer?

No passion so effectually robs the mind of all its powers of acting and reasoning as fear.

Edmund Burke

Why Women Find it Easier than Men to Discuss Their Fears

Rather than fleeing or fighting in response to stressful or fearful situations, women are more likely than men to seek social contact with other women and with their children. This is because of oxytocin, a chemical in the body that leads to maternal behaviour. Although both men and women produce it, its calming effects are reduced in men by the male hormone testosterone.

There is believed to be an evolutionary reason for this. As the traditional protector of children, a 'fight or flight' response would prevent women from shielding their children from impending danger. Instead, women developed a distinctive response that allows them to build relationships and form unions which help them protect their children. Researchers at UCLA have termed this new finding the 'tend and befriend' response. This calmer reaction, where adrenaline is not released in the same quantities as for 'fight or flight', may hold clues to why women, on average, live longer than men. Interestingly, researchers have shown that oxytocin is released in men when they bathe their babies and children, and that this can have positive relaxation and bonding benefits for both parents and children.

Harnessing the Power of a Fearful Encounter

The first step is to find and identify those first feelings of fear, the adrenaline drip. To do this exercise, think of something that makes you feel fearful. Perhaps a confrontation with your boss, filling in your tax return, a visit to a hospital, arguing with some-one over a parking space, or running out of money before the end of the month. Allow yourself to relive the situation for a moment, and answer the following questions:

1. How do you feel?
2. Where do you feel it (shoulders, back, stomach)?
3. What is your state of mind?

Now, think of a time when you were at your best, both mentally and physically. A time when you felt suffused with confidence, clarity and ability. Think of a couple of specific events in which you achieved great things. Maybe you sealed a deal, did well on an exam, convinced someone of your point of view, received praise for being a good listener, performed on stage and were applauded.

1. Write down the events in as much detail as you want.
2. Pick the most powerful event and imagine a circle on the floor just in front of your feet. I want you to imagine that this is your circle of power and confidence. Give it a colour. Seek out a colour that speaks of excellence and strength, a colour that you associate with happiness and mastery. Use all your senses to create a strong, positive, identifiable presence for this circle.
3. Imagine that within that circle is your powerful and positive past experience. Now, step forward into the circle and fully relive the experience. See what you saw, feel what you felt, and hear what you heard, making it bigger, brighter, bolder.
4. Step out of the circle for a moment. Then pick another powerful experience from the ones you've written down. Move back inside the circle and feel those wonderful affirming emotions all over again. Linger for a few moments.

5. Step back out. Now, step back in again and this time relive all the powerful positive experiences together. Feel strong, feel powerful.

6. Step out of the circle again. This time imagine that the circle contains a fearful experience from the first part of the exercise. But when you step back in you are taking with you all the positive feelings that you've been working on. See yourself in control of this fearful situation. Make it exactly as you'd like it to be.

Each and every one of us is basically a chemist. All the different feelings and emotions we have are different chemical cocktails mixed inside our own brains. Just as fear is a certain cocktail of chemicals, so are stress, and confidence, and happiness. The more often you practise accessing positive feelings, the more adept your brain will be at mixing them. This means you will easily be able to use them to your advantage when you are in a situation that would normally make you feel vulnerable.

He who fears being conquered is sure of defeat.

Napoleon Bonaparte

I work with lots of people who are scared of job interviews. They walk through the door and see the interviewers lined up behind the table, staring at them. Immediately they feel terrified. This is because they are reacting to what's represented by what they see in front of them. I work with them to help them control the controllables, so that before, during and after the interview they remain in a powerful, positive, but relaxed state. Bringing their own positive emotions through the door with them and remaining in control of those powerful feelings while they are being interviewed is one way to overcome their fears.

Use the exercise above to help train yourself to learn how to access powerful emotions as and when you want them, mixing your own chemicals of choice.

Taking Responsibility for Yourself

If you have a fear, you are skilful at being afraid. After all, you've invested a massive amount of time in perfecting your response. Chances are you've made it central to your life. You've shown enormous commitment. I know how much hard work goes into sustaining fear; it's completely exhausting. I worked with a (male) client who was afraid of talking to women. I said, 'Imagine you are going to employ me to "do" your fear for you. I'm working for an agency, and you're going on holiday next week. You're employing me to come in and do your fear for you.'

You have to expect things of yourself before you can do them.

Michael Jordan

He looked at me as if I were mad. But his incredulity was a clue to me about just how skilful he'd become at his fear. When you're that practised, it's second nature. He didn't really know how he did it. I pushed the point and it was then he began to explain. He would go to a bar where there were women. He'd look over and see an attractive woman, and immediately say to himself, 'Wow, she looks gorgeous, what chance have I got?' He would then spend a few minutes talking himself out of approaching her. Occasionally he'd go one step further and imagine himself approaching her: 'With each step my heart-rate increases. I'm breathing more and more deeply until, in my mind's eye, I'm sweating. The closer I get to her the bigger she seems to get, until she seems to be so Amazonian that she's towering over me. By the time I'm up close, feeling physically much smaller than her, my mouth is so dry I can't speak. I stutter; words fail me. Then she starts laughing out loud. Time slows down. Her laugh is very deep and distorted. Everyone is looking at me. I feel like I want to pass out.'

I told him that if that happened to me when I was in a room with women, I wouldn't go near them either.

This man had spent years avoiding situations because of what he feared *might* happen. Focusing on what might happen also meant that it was more likely to occur.

For many people, our fears have never actually happened. Instead, we have a feeling we are not good enough, or that we are ugly or boring, and our brain sets out to prove us right. This is a survival strategy. Fear is a product of the mind that emerges when your brain senses danger. However misguided that may be, your brain is only trying to protect you. There is nothing wrong with you; your brain is only trying to help you because it thinks it's for the best and doesn't know any better.

Everyone who has a fear or feels anxious has a way of going about it. It might be what you say to yourself, or something that you do.

Our fears are often no more than a way of thinking that we have practised until it becomes automatic, however small the threat to our safety really is. It's not my client's fault that a balloon went off in her face. It's not her fault that she then responded as if she were going to die every time she saw a balloon. What helped her was understanding what she was doing to herself, and choosing to respond in a different way.

Recently I had an MRI scan on a little lump (it was fine). The day before the scan a client came to me who happened to be very claustrophobic. I asked him to tell me how he 'did' his fear. He went into such detail about it that as I lay in the scanner I found myself remembering his words: 'You go into a small place and immediately you start shouting inside your head "how the hell am I going to get out?" and you start looking for an exit. If you can't find one, your breathing starts increasing and your heart starts going boomboomboomboom and you can feel your heart, and the voice in your head says "we're in trouble, we're going to die, ahhhhhh".' So I'm lying in the MRI scanner and I'm thinking, 'Don't think about that bloke,' which is like saying 'don't think about pink elephants.'

Adversity causes some men to break, others to break records.

William A. Ward

It's so easy to get caught up in other people's experiences. If I hadn't spent time thinking about being afraid of confined spaces the day before, I wouldn't have felt a drop of fear in the MRI scanner. The machine was no more or less frightening than it had ever been. But my *perception* of it had been altered, and that was enough to start producing sensations in me that felt real enough.

Ask yourself this: do you think you have a choice of whether or not to accept your brain's instructions?

You have, and you are not limited to doing what you have always done in the past. We might like to blame someone else or some particular set of circumstances for triggering our fears, but in order to conquer them we have to understand that we are the ones making ourselves frightened. All we have to do is take responsibility. And with willingness and openness to change comes the realization that your choices are limitless.

Exploring the way you 'do' your fear, and becoming familiar with the internal programme you are running and the resulting emotions, are the most effective ways to beginning to see fear through to the other side.

A Job Description of Your Fear

One of the exercises that I use to help people take control of their fear is to ask them to imagine that I'm from an employment agency. I'm coming in to do their job for them, so that they can have a break from it. They usually find this a bit strange, so I explain that in order for me to do their job/fear, they are going to have to teach me to do it.

This exercise allows people to step back from what they do. It is extremely effective because most people don't actually know how they 'do' their fear: it's automatic. They don't' realize, until they try this exercise, that their fearful reaction is actually a step-by-step process.

If you ask anyone who's extremely skilled at something how they do it, it's unlikely that they will be able to describe the process involved. If I were to ask Tiger Woods 'How do you swing that club so well?' it's unlikely that he'd know. He just does it effortlessly, and unconsciously, as a result of years of practise.

Asking someone to explain a process that is second nature is very challenging. If someone is very practised at something, explaining it will be difficult for them. You are challenging them to take something they do automatically and break it down into conscious elements.

Imagine learning how to walk or to drive a car again. To make these processes conscious again would probably result in you falling over or stalling the car. Do you remember how many things you had to do to learn to drive? Trying to think through all the tiny automatic decisions involved, to make it a conscious process again, would make driving a nightmare.

However, when it comes to breaking our patterns of fearful behaviour, this process is actually very helpful. Making the process of fear conscious again can have dramatic benefits, not least because it actually makes it harder to continue to engage in the fearful behaviour so effectively.

One woman I worked with had come to see me because she was so frightened of meeting men that she was terrified of talking to the opposite sex. She didn't even have to be in a room with them to start feeling frightened; just thinking about men was enough to make her scared.

The will to win is important, but the will to prepare is vital.

Joe Paterno

I said to her, 'Let's imagine that I'm going to come in tomorrow from a fear employment agency and do your fear for you. How do I do it, what do I do?' She looked at me with a dazed and confused expression, and said she didn't have a clue. Obviously she had become so highly skilled at doing her fear that she had no idea how she was going about it. After explaining what I was looking for, she was able to start briefing me on how to do her fear.

She said, 'If someone invites you to a party you immediately say to yourself, inside your head, "Oh my god, I hope there will be no men there."'

I heard this and started the process of breaking down her fear. I shouted, in a voice like a loud American soap actress, 'Oh. My. God. There are going to be loads of MEN there.' She looked a bit confused, but smiled and carried on describing her fear.

'The next thing you do is ask your friend, "Are there going to be lots of men there?"'

As she said this I noticed that her breathing had become faster and more shallow. I repeated her words back to her with the same loud, comically hysterical voice as before, but this time I was panting as if I'd just run up six flights of stairs.

Then she said that if her friend said that yes, there would be many men present: 'Immediately imagine yourself at the party completely surrounded by men, feeling absolutely terrified and trapped. Not knowing what to say, saying things inside your head like "They won't like me," "I'm so ugly," "I don't know what to say."'

I repeated her words in the same overblown way. This time she stopped in her tracks and allowed herself a broad smile. This was a great sign – it meant that she had begun the process of stepping back from her fear and was beginning to see it from a different perspective, as a well-rehearsed process.

She then explained, 'The longer the fear goes on in your mind, the smaller you get, and the bigger the men get. Soon you feel about three foot tall and realize you are surrounded by all these giants who are laughing and pointing their fingers at you. You just feel totally inadequate.'

At this point, after I mirrored back to her with great enthusiasm what she had told me, she started to laugh and said out loud, 'I can't believe I actually do that.'

I then asked her: 'Do you think this is an effective strategy for meeting men?'

She said that clearly it wasn't. So I asked her, 'So why do you do it?'

The exercise had made her aware that her fear was triggered when she played in her mind's eye a horrible movie, a series of terrifying images, pictures, thoughts and feelings that conspired to make her feel frightened.

Using a piece of A3 flip-chart paper, I then asked her to draw a chain and write the stages of her fear into the connected links she had sketched. Our fearful reactions are like a series of links on a chain, and sketching them helps us to see them from a fresh perspective.

I then asked her, 'Do you think you could break this chain at any point along it?'

If you can recognize when the fear begins, you can learn to break the first few chain links to stop the fear from spiralling out of control. You need to break the chain when you feel the process beginning, and do something else instead.

We then spent time going through a number of different simple exercises and strategies that she could use in order to break her chain of fear. These included telling that voice that initially asked 'Are there going to be any men there?' to shut up (see page 47); using her inner coach to help her remain positive and confident (see page 47); changing the pattern of her breathing (see page 85); and using imagery to help her focus on what she wants to have happen (see page 109).

After a couple of sessions, this woman felt confident enough to go to parties and start to mingle with men. She phoned me several months later to say that she had gone on a date with one man who was so self-opinionated and obnoxious that her confidence had taken a battering. 'Well, thank goodness you didn't marry him,' I said. Allow things to go wrong, but remember that success lies on the other side of failure.

Do you remember earlier on in the book when we spoke about you becoming a secret agent? Your new mission, should you choose to accept it – and, by the way, this page won't self-destruct in five seconds if you don't – is for you to become more aware of the process you go through when you become frightened of things. Then use some of the techniques in this book to help you break that cycle. The key to breaking any behavioural pattern is to learn to focus your attention on doing something else instead.

With the following exercise, you can either imagine you are asking someone to 'do' your fear for you, or you could ask a friend to help you. Either way, this exercise will help you learn to break down your fear and start focusing on doing something else. This will rob the fear process of much of its power over you. You'll be back in control, where you belong.

The only thing we have to fear is fear itself.

Franklin Delano Roosevelt

1. Imagine that you are employing someone to do your fear for you. Brief them on a job description of how to do your fear, labelling each stage of fear as an instruction. For example, rather than saying 'I feel this ...', say, 'You feel this ...'

2. If you are working with a friend, with each instruction that you give for how they should feel and what they should think, encourage them to say it back, just as I did with the woman above, making the statements sound as over-exaggerated and funny as possible.

If you think reliving the fear is going to be too intense, if you find yourself getting close to panic when you visualize what you go through, you might want to moderate the process slightly, using the approach shown below.

When Re-living Your Fear Is Too Much

This is a transcript of a real session I had with David, a man who suffered from panic attacks. His ability to visualize what happened to him the very first time he had suffered from an attack was so intense that I encouraged him to begin the process of changing his relationship to his fear in the act of telling it.

David: The first panic attack I had was 30 years ago. It was so terrifying. I look back at it as a crossroads in my life. I was in a woll-known hairdressing salon in London on a Saturday afternoon, millions of people everywhere.

Pete: OK, stop for a moment. Carry on telling me the story, but I want you to imagine that you are watching it as if it were on a cinema screen. You are over here, looking at someone who looks like you sitting in the hairdresser's chair. What happened to that person?

David: That person got incredibly hot. He felt he couldn't breathe.

Pete: And basically this person is a good-natured person?

David: Very.

Pete: And although he could have got up at any moment and said 'Look, I'm really hot, I need to get some fresh air,' he didn't.

David: Yes. Being the typically polite idiot that he is, he carried on.

Pete: So he got hotter and hotter and hotter.

David: That's right, until in the end it became unbearable.

Pete: So it's like putting your hand on a hot coal. You either keep it there or you pull it away because it hurts.

David: Absolutely, and he kept it in. It's ludricrous, the whole situation. I had my hair cut last week, and although it's nearly 30 years later, I'm still sitting in that chair relating to this outdated bunch of memories.

Pete: Imagine making the movie you are looking at black and white. Go on, drain it of colour. And while you're at it, imagine shifting it right over there to the far side of the room. So now, when you talk about it, it's beginning to seem like less of a problem.

When you are in danger of panicking about something, it helps to have played around with a movie of your fear beforehand. Then, when the situation arises, concentrate on shifting the image away from you, watching yourself on a movie screen, turning down the volume, making the image black and white and grainy. These are all ways to deflate the 'boom'.

A few months later David told me that for the first time in 30 years he'd had a haircut without feeling frightened. 'I knew that if I wanted to I could get up and walk out of the salon, I also realized that feeling frightened was something I could choose *not* to feel, so I didn't,' he said.

Space – The Only Frontier

I went to visit a good friend in the countryside recently. As soon as I had dropped my bags inside his cottage he said, 'I want to take you somewhere.' He's done this before, so I knew when he said that he was about to take me somewhere beautiful. He lives on the South Downs, and we walked outside the cottage and up a pathway snaking up the hill behind his cottage. We walked to a large field where we could gaze over the Downs, across open, rolling agricultural land for miles and miles. The wind was blowing in wisps, the sky was blue, the sun was beaming. All was quiet. I felt all the stresses of my week just fade away. As we stood there, wordlessly, I realized that I was entirely surrounded by the natural world.

The experience of overcoming fear is extraordinarily delightful.

Bertrand Russell

What is so important about the natural world? Well, the only reason we're on this earth is because of it. The Chinese have always known about the importance of nature and what they term the elements: earth, fire, air, wood, water. The only reason we are all on this earth is because of these ancient elements; remove one of them and there is no life. When I was recently travelling in China, everywhere you go from crack of dawn, you see people practising the ancient martial art of T'ai Chi. All they are doing is energizing themselves by exercising outdoors, in the elements.

What has this got to do with you? To get over your fear, it's important that you give yourself space and nourishment, and perhaps one of the best ways to do this is to find time to go outside, look around and be with nature.

We need nourishment in our lives, whether it's looking at a beautiful view, lying in a hot bath, reading a book or relaxing in a hammock.

In a study of depression several years ago, a psychologist told a group of depressed people that they would not actually start the therapy for two weeks. He told them that all he wanted them to do for the next two weeks in preparation for the therapy was to go out every day and see how many chimneys they could find. Whether you realize it or not, people who are frightened, depressed and worried tend to have a lot of self-talk or indulge in a lot of self-analysis. This invariably involves looking downwards and inwards. After two weeks, without knowing what they were doing or why they were doing it, the depressed people in the study had radically changed their physiology, which in turn had radically changed their mood. Just the process of looking up and out had the power to change everything.

Happiness Tonic

1. Look up now at the sky, and smile. Try to feel frightened.
2. Imagine you can see laughter inside your head, hundreds of people laughing and cheering happily. Now try and feel frightened.

The best and perhaps the hardest mission in life is to be responsible for the way you feel in each moment. You can start to breathe more fully. You can start to enjoy yourself much more. You can stop rushing to get somewhere, enjoying the process of getting there, rather than focusing exclusively on what is to come. Learn to savour each moment of your very precious life. Life doesn't last for ever.

Being 99

1. Imagine you are 99 years old, and looking back over your life. What would you wish you had done less of? Write down two or three things here. Examples could include being less critical, less worrying, less self-destructive behaviour.
2. If you were 99 years old now, what would you wish you had done more of? Write some of them down here. Examples might be travelling more, laughing more, having had more fun.

The joy is that you are probably not 99 years old yet. Look at your list of things you wish you'd done more of. If these are things you really want to do, you still have time to do them. Look at your list of dislikes. It's not too late to stop now. What's stopping you? You. And only you can decide to do things differently.

Many of the people I've worked with who have started to do more of the things they've wanted to do, and fewer of the things they don't like, have eventually had little or no time to be frightened – they are too busy doing things they enjoy.

A Short Note about Imperfection

You might give yourself a hard time over things you don't enjoy, such as being in a crowd or knowing the right thing to say. Allow yourself to be less than perfect. Don't beat yourself up about your failings. Instead, accept that these are not areas of strength for you. Avoid them if you can, and if you can't, just observe what is going on around and within you. Let your inner coach come on side, reassuring you that it won't last much longer and you're coping well, given how difficult this is for you.

The most wonderful quality you can foster is to be gentle with yourself. Everything else will then take care of itself. When you're in the bath, you're being gentle with yourself. When you watch light filtering through a blind, you're being gentle with yourself. When you support and encourage yourself when you are having difficulties, you are being gentle with yourself.

They can conquer who believe they can.

John Dryden

Find something that makes you feel relaxed and happy – perhaps driving, walking, hugging someone you love, watching the sky, baking a cake or lying warmly under the covers on a Saturday morning. Next time you do this thing, really listen to your internal reactions. I want to encourage you to take that sense of your own space with you wherever you go. It's fully portable. If you lose the feeling, make sure you step back and recharge it when you can.

Nurturing Belief in Your Own Power

If someone is resistant to you, one of the best things you can do is to meet their resistance with gentleness. This is not for their benefit, but for yours. It's not always easy. I could be giving a workshop and someone could really disagree with me, and get quite personal about it. The temptation is to react to them. But it is in being able to disengage, step back and observe the other person where true strength lies. If someone is being really objectionable to you, don't react or get wound up. Instead, just think to yourself 'Thank God I'm not you' – or better still, 'Thank God I don't have to be with you every day.' There is no point wasting energy becoming angry or upset when it's clear no resolution can be found.

Many of us want to know ourselves and to feel whole and accepted. Unfortunately, we tend to go about looking in the wrong direction, seeking self-knowledge and acceptance externally through objects, money and other people. In English there is no word for this craving for acceptance. 'Unconditional love' is the closest we have to it. In Japanese it is called *amaru*, which means 'to rest secure in loving arms, to presume upon the love given by another person'. It's a sense of snuggling up to unconditional support. We long for *amaru*, but it takes confidence, because it raises the fear of abandonment. We also need to strike a balance. You can't rely on it all the time, and some people want it too much. They look to other people for validation and to provide them with positive feelings. We tend to forget that our most infinite and endless resource is placing ourselves within the support and security of our own embrace.

How Up for Change Are You?

I once gave a presentation to the senior staff of one of the world's biggest companies. I love being on stage, it's a big joy for me. I have a way of doing things, usually on my own, but on this occasion I was working with Sally Gunnell, the former Olympic and world champion, and I had to shift my approach a bit, which was a big challenge for me. A running track had been constructed on the stage. Sally ran on and said, 'To help me with my presentation today I've got a friend, Pete Cohen.' Now, these people didn't know me. They could have had all kinds of expectations of me. But if I started to focus on their expectations I would be in big trouble. There was only one thing I could do. My challenge was to enjoy what I was doing, regardless of the result. Sally said it was the same for her when she was competing; she had to focus on herself. If she focused on all the things that could go wrong, if she focused on the opposition, she would immediately be weakened.

The presentation went so well that I was invited back on my own, a year later. One of the directors asked me if I could really motivate his staff. Motivating people and gearing them up is easy for me, but what difference does that make if you can't teach people to motivate themselves? As the expression goes, 'give a man a fish and you feed him for a day, but teach him to fish and you feed him for a lifetime.' I don't want these people to listen to me talk for an hour and feel motivated for just a few hours afterwards. I want them to learn to motivate themselves. So I asked the director a question: 'How do you want these people to feel when I've finished talking?' He replied, 'I don't know.' I asked him to think about it and call me back when he could tell me. Three days later he called me back and said, 'I want them to feel that they can really make a difference, and that if they roll their sleeves up they can help make this company and all of us working in it successful.' It was at this point that I stopped him for a moment and asked him, 'What do you think stops people from rolling up their sleeves?' He wasn't sure, so I asked him another question: 'What are some of the habits that some of your employees have that stop them from being more productive, and in turn rolling up their sleeves?' He then reeled them off, 'Not focusing on what they are doing, trying to do too many things in one go, moaning and complaining, not taking pride in what they are doing, never finishing the job properly ...' the list went on. I then explained to him that his employees had probably invested a lot of time and energy into these unproductive behaviours, that these behaviours had become second nature to most of them. Because of the investment they'd made, getting them to step out of their comfort zones would be a huge challenge.

Who bravely dares must sometimes risk a fall.

Tobias George Smollett

I've worked with Sally on many occasions since then. Our presentations are not about teaching businesses how to make more money. Our goal is to share with organizations the power of enjoying what you do, so their employees get up every day and say, 'I can't wait to go to work.'

This is the challenge we all face. Just to enjoy what we are doing and leave unproductive habits behind. If you're enjoying something, you're much more likely to be effective. And if someone doesn't like you, that's their problem.

Feedback tells me that my presentations usually go down well, and people are affected by what I say. However, there are always those who do not really take on board what I have to say, and choose not to change. Many of us don't want to change because we're actually more comfortable where we are. It's sad that we live in a world where many people don't want to change, even if they are unhappy. The questions I have for you are, 'Do you want to change, and what are you prepared to do about it?'

How Can I Overcome My Fears for Good?

The future is now. If you can start to enjoy what you are doing on a day-to-day basis, the future will take care of itself. It's as simple as that, although that's a big leap of faith for most people to take, used as we are to directing and investing so much of our attention away from the present moment.

If there is something that you want to happen in the future, worrying about it not happening is the most counter-productive approach possible. Instead, just make a picture of what you do want to happen and push your attention back to the present moment. Remember, wishes are very powerful, and be careful what you wish for.

How Long Will It Take?

Some of your fears were learned when you were young and impressionable. You learned to react in a certain way back then, and as time has gone on this behaviour has developed and become well-rehearsed. People believe that because they've had their fears for such a long time, they're always going to have them. But the fact is that you have it within your power to stop being frightened *immediately*. You can do this by choosing to focus your attention somewhere else.

I recently saw someone who was frightened of ruining her relationship. Although it was the best relationship she'd ever had, she was worried that she was going to mess it up. She wanted to have children, but she didn't know how to be certain whether she was with the right man for the long haul.

One thing is for certain in this woman's case: If she continues to spend time constantly analysing whether this is the right person the relationship is not going to grow. By allowing herself to worry constantly, she is already influencing events negatively. Instead she needs to focus her attention on enjoying the relationship. This will allow her to take her attention away from her fears and onto the good parts of the relationship itself. She will soon find out whether the relationship is nourishing or not.

Your Own World of Fear

People often think that a relationship is the answer to all their problems. 'If I could just find the right person, everything would be all right.' What they actually believe is that someone else can make their lives better for them. Unfortunately, life doesn't always work like this. If you have lots of insecurities which you haven't addressed, chances are they will surface in your relationships. If you find your own life hard, if you struggle and have lots of negative thoughts, you may want to ask yourself this question: Is there room for another person? You might end up projecting all your fears onto them and thinking the other person is at fault when really these are your own demons.

We often think we'll be OK as soon as we get certain things: a good relationship, a new car, a better job, lots of attention. But those things are all outside ourselves.

Who is responsible for your feelings? For your fear? For your happiness? Is it someone else, or is it you?

The Challenge of Change

Don't expect to receive unconditional support when you start making changes in your life. We all have images of how people are. To us, how they are is *who* they are. If you start changing, you will no longer be fulfilling quite the same role that you represent in other people's minds. That can be quite frightening for them. And also for you.

My client David was really up for change. In our session he was lapping up ways to control his panic attacks. He told me of the support he knew he would receive back at home. 'I am lucky because I live with a very calm person indeed, and the only thing we fall out about is my aggression. She thinks I am a very aggressive person indeed, and it's true, my panic attacks make me aggressive.'

'David,' I said. 'What are you going to do when you are no longer aggressive? What are you going to do with the time you have spent worrying?'

The brave man is not he who feels no fear, for that were stupid and irrational; but he whose noble soul subdues its fear, and bravely dares the danger nature shrinks from.

Joanna Baillie

David considered my question for a moment. 'Sure, I can see that I've got to find other things to do. I can't turn all this into something of real use and value if I don't work out what I'm going to do instead.'

Future Beyond Fear

Spend a moment to consider what would be different in your life as a consequence of changing. It might help you to write down some answers to the following questions.

1. What are you going to do when you are no longer ruled by this fear?
2. What are you going to do with all the time you used to spend being frightened?
3. If you were free from your fear, what would be different on a day-to-day basis?
4. How would your life change?
5. What would you get out of being different?
6. What would it give you?
7. What would it take away?

Don't Create Another World of Fear

The worst of poisons: to mistrust one's power.

Heinrich Heine

You have practised being the way you are for so long, that when you start changing there is a temptation to say, 'Hang on, I don't do my life like that.'

I had a session with a man who was terrified of flying. The following week he felt really good, but he told me that the week after that he went back to feeling frightened of flying. 'I don't normally feel OK about flying. The change is a bit strange and I'm not sure how to deal with it.'

It is so easy for your mind to go off and have familiar, fearful thoughts. You've practised your fear for so long, after all. If you find your mind constantly drifting back to fearful thoughts and feelings, engage your mind in something else. Plant a garden in your imagination with countless tasks and creative challenges to meet. Make it play the perfect game of golf. Count the odd sheep if you have to.

Our minds often drift into the fear zone when we are trying to get to sleep. This is because we are not being stimulated by anything else. If you start feeling the fear then, or at any time, tell your inner coach to encourage your mind to go back to the imaginative task you set it.

As children we escape the mundane moments in life by using our imagination. When I was at school and bored by a particularly dull and uncharismatic teacher, I coped by letting myself drift off into another world. Let yourself day-dream with images that make you feel good, happy and liberated.

In a more physical way, you will also benefit from engaging your mind in something practical. Learn French. Take up gardening for real. Put some energy into doing new things, things that nourish you and make you feel good, whether it's walking, exercising, reading or spending more time with your children. Consider doing something you have never done before, such as travelling more, painting or taking up diving.

If you don't give yourself something to do when you are moving on from fear, the chances are your brain will just go and find some more fear for you to do. This is particularly true if you've had a lot of fear in your life.

How many people develop a fear of flying halfway into a 12-hour flight when they've got nothing else to do? Research into this phenomenon was precisely why airlines learned to offer us entertainment options, such as films and music. Even on a short flight we are offered drinks, snacks, magazines and other distractions.

What to Do If You Are Nervous about Flying

I see a lot of people who are frightened of flying. Our bodies are not designed to be travelling along at altitude inside a pressurized tube with wings, and the events of 11 September 2001 have only intensified these fears. However much we tell ourselves these fears are projections inside our head, they still feel real.

Try the following visualization to help you overcome your fear. You can apply this to any stressful situation, tailoring it to your own fear. You can even record it and listen to it as often as you like.

1. Sit quietly and imagine watching on a big cinema screen someone who looks a lot like you going to an airport. This

person is very calm, really collected and very cool. They look like an old hand at flying, someone for whom flying is as normal as taking a bus.

2. You check in, get on the plane whistling away to yourself, and during take-off you marvel at the wonders of modern technology.

3. The flight is over in a flash, the plane lands and you watch yourself getting off feeling well rested.

4. Imagine yourself on holiday doing all the things you love. Imagine the sea, the sun, the warm air, the sights and sounds, the food you love to eat.

5. Now imagine the holiday's over and it's time to come home. You fly back with a wonderful sense of all that you have seen and done. You land, get into your car and travel back home fuelled with the wonderful memories of your holiday.

6. Breathe deeply and imagine that you are no longer just watching a cinema screen showing a travel specialist who looks like you. Instead you are stepping into the image and arriving at an airport deeply relaxed. There is no one else on earth as relaxed as you and as excited about your trip. This is your imagination and you can have things just the way you want them.

7. You are feeling what it is like to be in control of your breathing, full of anticipation, joy and peace as the plane takes off.

8. You go up, up, up. You are in the sky, relishing the wonderment of being above the land, amazed that you are able to travel to the other side of the world so easily.

9. The plane lands, you get off and go on holiday in your mind. Feel the sensations. The food, the landscape, the weather. Paint a mental picture of being in your favourite destination.

10. Imagine stepping back on to the plane with an overwhelming sense of joy and happiness.

11. Imagine coming back, and this time there is a bit of turbulence and you breathe deeply, and imagine that because you are breathing deeply the turbulence stops. The plane lands and you return home, deeply refreshed.

12. Let your inner coach congratulate you. For somebody who has a problem, you are remarkably calm and going about this in a very nourishing way. You are very good at this, aren't you? You have a very strong imagination. It's easy for you to picture this.

Next time you need to get on a plane, here are ways to cope.

When you're afraid, it's natural to stop in your tracks. Yet the longer you stay stopped, the more you'll begin to feel frozen, a feeling that will intensify your fears. Occupy or distract yourself with a book or conversation. Absorb yourself in reading or talking and you'll send a message to your brain that you are not 'stuck', whereupon you'll begin to feel more calm. Talking to your neighbours will also relax them a little, and some of this is likely to rub off on you.

Take slow and deep breaths. Just changing your breathing pattern can change how you feel. Taking deep breaths through your nose helps to release a little tension with each exhalation.

If you don't know what you're doing today, how do you know if you're going to do something different tomorrow?

Blake Wilder

Learning to Relax

Leading a long and healthy life is all about staying cool, calm and collected whatever situation you are in.

There are admirable potentialities in every human being. Believe in your strength and your youth. Learn to repeat endlessly to yourself: 'It all depends on me.'

Andre Gide

It's only human to continue to act in ways we've practised over time, whether or not they are the most appropriate or effective ways to behave. This applies even to the most basic process of all, breathing. Some people won't believe that changing something as simple as the way they breathe can be so effective in helping them deal with fear.

The only way you can relax is to breathe deeply. There is no other way.

Unfortunately, most of the time we do not breathe in a way that nourishes us. When you are confronted by fear or anxiety, one of the first ways your body responds is by altering the way you are breathing. Your breath becomes shallow and speeds up until you are hyper-ventilating. It is almost impossible to stay calm and in control when you are breathing like this.

This disturbed, panicky pattern of breath causes us to fail to take in enough oxygen. This sends a message through our whole body that we are facing an emergency.

Therefore, the first response to fear should be a long, deep breath. This will nourish every system in your body with oxygen and send a message to your brain that the threat is passing. Take a deep breath through your nose, right now. It's very difficult to feel stressed and anxious while doing that, isn't it?

What we vividly imagine, ardently desire, enthusiastically act upon, must inevitably come to pass.

Colin Pesission

If you watch a small baby, whether awake or asleep, you will notice that not only does her chest rise, but also her stomach. A baby fills almost all her lung space with air as she breathes, ensuring that her body is being continuously oxygenated. Babies are naturally deep breathers. As the diaphragm is pulled downwards, the lungs automatically inflate, and you can see this movement in the stomach.

As people get older they tend to become lazy in their breath and their breathing becomes more shallow. They flex their diaphragm just a tiny amount and use only a fraction of their lung capacity to push oxygen into their system. This means they need to breathe more frequently to extract an equivalent amount of oxygen.

The problem is that speeding up your breath sends a message to your body that you have a small emergency on. This means that even if you are not feeling fearful, this rapid breathing pattern can itself trigger the release of adrenaline, fooling your body into thinking you are facing some kind of crisis and keeping you in a state of stress.

You have the power literally to breathe yourself into anxiety. You also have the power to arrest this process.

In order to combat your fear, you need to tackle it on more than one level. Up until now, we have addressed your fear on an emotional level. Now I want to help you go one step further, by helping you change what you do with your body.

Breathe Yourself Calm

1. Right now, take three long slow deep breaths, breathing in through your nose and out through your nose or mouth.
2. As you slowly exhale, encourage your inner coach to say the word 'calm' in your mind.
3. As you continue to breathe slowly and deeply, expand your awareness of the space in front of you. And above you. Behind and beneath you. Become more aware of your space with every slow, nourishing breath.
4. Become aware of the difference between an inhalation and an exhalation, and focus on the process.

5. Increase the effect by inhaling the colour that best works for you. Fill yourself up with a colour that energizes and feeds you.

6. Notice how you feel.

Breathing puts you deeply in touch with what's really around you. It gets you out of your head and draws your focus back into your body. It's peaceful. You immediately feel more relaxed and life slows down. What's more, breathing through your nose brings a cascade of scents to your attention, something you miss out on when you breathe through your mouth. Simple things can be so effective.

Energy follows thought.

Julie Soskin

If you find it difficult to breathe deeply, right into the bottom of your lungs, the following exercise will help you in your daily life. By practising it regularly you will be able to use it immediately when faced by your fear.

Learning to Breathe Deeply

1. Lie down comfortably with your back on the floor.
2. Place a book on your stomach.
3. As you breathe in through your nose, allow the book to rise.
4. As you breathe out, allow the book to sink towards your stomach. Do this for as long as you feel comfortable.

5. See how deep your breaths can become, how much you can move the book, how relaxed you can be. Count your breaths if that helps you focus more clearly on them.
6. Breathe in an enriching colour, as before.
7. Keep breathing like this for a minute or so.
8. Slowly stand up. Begin to put this deep breathing consciously into practice in your daily life. This will make it easier to recognize the benefits and use the technique whenever you are faced with a stressful or anxiety-inducing situation.

If you are suffering from tension, want to drain it off rapidly and can't lie down, try the following suggestion.

Push Push

1. Stand upright with your knees slightly bent.
2. Forcefully push through the air around you with your open hands at abdomen level, first to one side hand and then to the other.
3. Exhale forcibly with each push with a strong 'huh, huh' sound. Do this a couple of times and you'll feel the tension dissipating.

Another technique, this time drawn from the martial art Aikido, can help you eradicate stress on demand.

Dissolving Stress

1. Stand tall, close your eyes, straighten your spine and relax.
2. Become aware of your breathing, and make sure it is deep and slow.
3. Place the index finger of your left hand on your navel, and slide the next finger down 2 inches below this point.
4. Remove your finger from your navel and keep a very light pressure on the point below it. This is called *hara*.
5. As you breathe out, visualize stress leaving your body through this channel. Choose a colour for it, a colour that you would like to purge, to make this an even more effective technique.

For instant control over your breathing, pick a favourite tune and sing or whistle it continuously. This is a simple way to control your breathing and calm yourself down.

Change is happening in and around us all the time. We grow new cells, we learn new ideas, the seasons turn and the weather is never what you expected. So open up to changes and changes will happen.

Learning to Change Your State

Our states can change very rapidly. A baby can go from blissful smiles to disgruntled crying in just a moment, and adults too can experience lightning-quick changes of state. If you hear a police siren you instantly become alert and your attention travels to the source of the noise. When you hear your name called, you prick up your ears and your head spins towards the person addressing you. Someone you love enters the room and your heart-rate changes. A piece of music can transport you into a rhapsodic trance.

Great martial artists are able to go into whichever state they want, whenever they want. I once saw a demonstration of martial artist monks who were displaying their mental strength by lying on beds of nails and doing somersaults in the air. These people have learned how to put their attention into the strongest part of their body, their centre – and they can do so instantly.

In contrast, I once worked with a British champion judo player. He had learned his sport in England, rather than in the East where this martial art originated. He was always self-critical and focused on what he was doing wrong. He thought negatively and constantly analysed his mistakes. I couldn't believe that someone so negative and self-defeating had actually become British champion. But through asking him a series of questions it became apparent why he'd won his last tournament to become champion. Having lost the previous seven or eight contests, he'd gone into this championship with a mentality that said, 'I've got nothing to lose.' People who say this to themselves always have everything to gain. He removed all pressure and expectations from himself in that moment, and simply enjoyed the competition for itself, something he hadn't done for years. We can all learn from this.

In the East, martial artists are taught to focus not on their heads, where fears start, but in the centre of their body where they believe their energy comes from. They call this energy *chi*, and they believe it comes from the area around their navel. By shifting their focus to this point, they stop analysing and start to feel strong.

I've been continuing to work with the judo player using this idea, and he has continued to enjoy success. But more importantly, he's enjoying his sport for the first time.

Buddhist monks learn first to meditate in quiet, peaceful locations. As they mature they practise meditation in noisy places. The lesson they are learning is not to be affected by their external environment, by things outside themselves. The golfer Tiger Woods is a master at focusing on his internal world. If he shifted his attention into the crowd he would be far less effective. Instead, he focuses on his own state, despite what is going on around him, and stuns us all. He's got a great inner coach working on his side, helping to put him into a positive space.

Many of us find it difficult to manage our states because we've developed so many mental comfort zones. We've become used to, even comfortable with, being anxious, frightened or stressed.

I want to encourage you to be responsible for your own state. I want you to imagine that you're setting up your own company. Your company only has one role. It's mission statement is to manage your state. To be responsible for how you think and act. Your inner coach is your only employee, and you give him or her complete control of supporting you and running your business. This is all about your ability to focus on enjoying your life, regardless of what's going on around you.

It is not because things are difficult that we do not dare, it is because we do not dare that they are difficult.

Seneca

Becoming a State Manager

You'll need a friend on hand for this exercise, and to get maximum benefit from it I suggest you remove your shoes, which will help you feel more grounded.

1. To begin the process, imagine you have a small tennis-sized ball in the centre of your body. Breathe into that part of your body and feel strong.
2. Stand straight up with your eyes on the horizon and your feet 8 inches apart. Unlock your knees, keeping them very slightly bent.
3. Find the point on your lower stomach that is about three finger-width spaces below your belly-button. Press a finger on that point and, as you take it away, relax completely and put your attention there.
4. Breathe into this part of your body, allowing all thoughts to just drift away.
5. Imagine filling your body up with a colour that you associate with strength and relaxation.
6. Become aware of the space all around you. The space in front, the space behind, above, below, to the left, to the right.
7. Now think of a time when you've felt frightened, but keep your focus of attention on your stomach and the space

around you. Begin to notice that it's difficult to think about your fear in the same way when you come from a position of strength. In this state many people's fears become insignificant and are not seen as a problem any more.

Practise this every day for a few weeks. Practise keeping your attention in your stomach when people are talking to you.

When you need to feel more in control, or the next time you are confronted by your fear, just switch your focus from your mind to that point below your naval. Your ability to face whatever difficulty you confront will automatically become easier.

We spend so much of our time with our attention directed inside our heads, preoccupied with worries. And we wonder why we often feel wobbly and out of control.

Rocking to Get a Grip

Do you remember when you were a baby and cried at night? Chances are your mother or father would pick you up and gently rock you gently until you fell asleep. Do you remember when you were a child going on a rocking horse or a swing? Do you understand the appeal of a hammock on a tropical holiday? Why do you think rocking chairs remain popular? Rocking has wonderful physiological benefits. It quiets the mind and relaxes the body. I used to work with children with severe emotional, learning and behavioural difficulties, and I noticed they would spend time rocking themselves. I asked their carers why they were rocking, and it was explained to me that this movement was the children's way of giving themselves some control over their minds.

I've used rocking as a way of helping hundreds of people overcome their fears and phobias. Again, this is not something you have to believe in, but it's something that I recommend that you try. Right now, as you continue to read this book, just gently rock backwards and forwards in your seat.

It's how you get there and the company you keep that determines the shape you're in when you arrive.

Sasha Moran

Rocking Yourself to Serenity

1. Stand up with your feet 6 inches apart. Focus on breathing deeply into your stomach. Then, very slowly, rock forwards on to your toes and then back on to your heels. Do this slowly and continue to focus on your breathing.
2. Repeat at least seven times. Become aware of the space all around you – above, below, in front, behind, to your right and to your left.

Practise this exercise as often you can, whether seated or standing. Eventually you will be able to do this inside your mind, without actually moving at all.

Rocking has the power to make you feel very calm on demand. It's another simple strategy that is very effective.

9

Taking Control

Why do you think so few people in life truly excel? Consider the men and women who reach the pinnacle of business and commerce, those who top the music charts, the actors and actresses who consistently win the best roles, or those in sport with Olympic gold. Why is it that there are only a handful at the top of their respective professions?

As a man thinks, so does he become.

Cervantes

The difference between those who make it and those who don't is the same as that which distinguishes those who succeed in conquering their fear and those who don't. The difference is an attitude that accepts nothing short of complete success.

If, instead of feeling a sense of impending failure when contemplating overcoming your fear, you can learn to feel a sense of impending achievement, your motivation to succeed, and your belief that you can, will automatically increase. You can learn to see and think in different ways, and to expect different things. Just like those who reach the top all the time.

A natural tendency when you are worried is to talk to yourself. Your inner critic says 'I can't do this' or 'This is never going to work.' This is, in its way, an affirmation, but not a very positive one. In fact, it doesn't do anything for you at all. The champion judo player I worked with had come for help because he was frightened of losing, and was always talking to himself in a negative way.

An affirmation is something you repeat in your head that leads to a change in your mood. The states you end up in after a fearful affirmation are not particularly helpful.

Instead, encourage your inner coach to support you when you are worrying. When you are fearful, you really want to get yourself into a strong and confident state.

Find an affirmation that works best for you. This is a phrase to say in your mind that encourages you to concentrate on what you are doing, helps you unwind, and stops you from focusing on things that might never happen.

Try the following:

- ⊘ 'I'm a winner.'
- ⊘ 'I'm focused.'
- ⊘ 'I'm powerful.'
- ⊘ 'I'm gorgeous.'
- ⊘ 'I'm ready.'
- ⊘ 'I'm on top of the world.'
- ⊘ 'I can do anything.'

Focusing on these positive phrases pulls you away from the stress reflex (quick breathing and cold, clammy hands) and towards a more powerful state. The result is that you calm down.

Write down your own personal affirmation. It can be one from the list above, or be one specific to you.

Saying your affirmation *out loud* gives you even greater power over your state. A great example of this is the 'Haka', the dance and incantation used by the New Zealand rugby team, which is based on an ancient Maori warrior tradition. The movement each member of the team makes helps put them into a very strong, fired-up state that helps them to see through the opposition and become totally focused on themselves. A by-product of the dance is that it instils a sense of fear into the opposition because the team look so collectively united and so individually strong. The other team have two choices: they can watch or look away, while the Kiwis gain in power.

Saying words out loud can make some people feel silly and uncomfortable. If you're not used to talking to yourself this way, it might feel a bit strange at first. But successful people do this as a matter of course. It's second nature to them.

Get into the habit of beginning and ending your day by looking in the mirror and repeating your affirmation. Do it whenever you catch sight of your reflection, or when you need to motivate yourself for a particular task. See what a difference it makes, both to your behaviour and your attitude towards and about yourself. Remember, you are the only one who can give yourself self-confidence.

Go confidently in the direction of your dreams, live the life you've imagined.

Henry David Thoreau

Think of some of the professional sportspeople you may watch on television. Many of them make specific sounds or movements before and during the event. They do this because, having practised over and over again, they have come to know the result these sounds or movements will produce. Some players call these superstitions, but they are always done with the intention of putting them into a positive state.

Harnessing the Power of Power-moves

When I work with sportspeople, I often find that they have developed a piece of specific behaviour for just before a race, match or competition. They might always get changed in the same part of the changing room, or touch their head a certain number of times. This helps them to focus. I encourage them to embrace the idea behind this and find an even more effective way of getting into a positive state: using a trigger word or a 'power move'.

Usually people who experience extreme fears can identify what it is that triggers their fear. For them, just thinking about the trigger can stimulate a spiral of terror. But you can also use this same principle to create a new trigger of your very own, one that will put you into a very resourceful state rather than a fearful one.

In an episode of a television science programme, a group of people were shown how to *imagine* themselves exercising. They were told they had to imagine themselves doing this three times a week for 12 weeks. After 12 weeks, all of the participants had increased their muscle tone without doing any actual exercise at all. All the exercise was in their mind.

How does this work? Well, when you imagine your muscles working, your brain sends a message through your nervous system and into your muscles. You don't feel it, but your muscles start working inperceptibly. Constant repetition of all the tiny movements are consolidated, and the muscle is actually toned. This demonstrates how powerful the mind is.

Verbalizing this kind of positive thinking makes it even more effective.

The next exercise is about really stepping out of your comfort zone, and going for it. It's often used by professional athletes.

Power-move

1. Imagine yourself the way you want to be, whether that's incredibly relaxed, really calm or full of energy and confidence.
2. Visualize your imaginary circle, as you did earlier. It's on the ground in front of you, just inches away from your toes.
3. When you step into that circle you are going to feel exactly how you want to feel. Step into it now, and make it a really confident stride. Don't make it a nervous little step; put some power and energy into it. As you do so, repeat your affirmation out loud or in your head.
4. Project your colour into the circle. Step in and out a few times.
5. Step back out, and as you step back in feel how much stronger you feel this time.
6. Step back out again, and this time I want you to think of a movement you can make to emphasize your commitment

to change, to feeling the way you want to feel. This is your power-move, and it will act like a trigger to remind you how fantastic you felt in the circle. Some people make a fist and punch the air, or draw it into their waist as they would on having achieved a sought-after goal. Find some physical movement that for you reinforces the feeling *'I can.'*

7. Try doing it now. As you step into the circle again – with a really energetic, confident stride – make your power-move. Doing this in a half-hearted way just won't work.

8. Try it a few times. Then as you step confidently into the circle, making your power move, I'd like you to think or say your affirmation. If you say it out loud, make a really big noise. The louder the better.

9. Try this a few times, before remaining in your circle and letting positive feelings wash over you.

10. When you step out for the last time, imagine shrinking that circle of power down to the size of a bracelet and putting it on your wrist.

    Whenever you need a shot of confidence or focus, squeeze this 'bracelet' and get your inner coach to say your affirmation. Allow yourself to have relaxed, confident feelings every time.

Watch your thoughts, they become words. Watch your words, they become actions. Watch your actions, they become habits. Watch your habits, they become your character. Watch your character, it becomes your destiny.

Frank Outlaw

With practice, you'll find that every time you make your power-move, you can step directly into the state you want to be in.

Once you have done this exercise a few times at home and are skilled at it, you can do it almost anywhere, although you don't have to say the affirmation out loud. Repetition enforces the message, so the more you can do it, the better.

How to Control a Panic Attack

'Your body feels like it is malfunctioning,' says David, who suffered panic attacks for nearly 30 years. 'Shortness of breath. Palpitations. A racing heart. Feeling faint. It affects your life physically, emotionally and practically.'

If you suffer panic attacks, you have an awful existence. You are constantly vigilant to the possibility of another attack. You live your life avoiding the things that you fear will trigger one, because the very idea is so unspeakably terrifying.

Says Gillian: 'When I was five someone pushed a pillow over my face for a joke. It put something in me; night fears, a terror of the pitch black room. I would dream I was awake and had opened my eyes but couldn't see.' Things got worse over the next 30 years.

In October 2001, I fell asleep in a window seat in the sitting room at home. I woke up and saw only blackness. I felt like I had been buried alive. The panic started setting in. Where was I? Where was my family? As my heart-rate increased I became convinced that they had deserted me and I was bricked in. All I could see was blackness. It was so real. I realized I needed air. If I didn't get air I was going to suffocate. I put my hands on the window above me, hyperventilating, desperate to breathe. The panic was overriding everything. With the palm of my hand I smashed the pane of glass. I can remember the cool air gushing in. I took deep, deep breaths. Then I realized I could see outside. I wasn't bricked in at all. I started coming to my senses and sat down, shocked, wondering what the hell I had just done. I realized I needed help.

A panic attack is like being trapped in a scary movie. Panic attacks know few boundaries, and a huge number of people experience these terrifying feelings. You feel a lack of control that seems to accelerate, speeding you towards a crescendo of fear. You get more and more frightened of what is happening. As your body pumps out adrenaline you breathe increasingly quickly, which in turn pumps out more adrenaline. Soon, you are panting rapidly; your breathing is very shallow and the air barely has a chance to circulate before it is rapidly expelled. You stop processing oxygen and carbon dioxide properly, so within moments you are struggling with light-headness and a fear that you might collapse. Having such strong sensations wash over you and feeling powerless to stop them is very, very frightening.

Because of their intensely terrifying nature, it is easy to become extremely fearful of panic attacks, and the temptation is to do anything to avoid them. But there is another way. You don't have to accept that your life is ruled by fear. As with other fearful reactions, the key is in knowing how to effectively change the focus of your attention. You may feel powerless to stop a panic attack, but in fact you *can* take control.

I once worked with a man called Bobby who suffered intensely from panic attacks for many years, but who has now freed himself from these dreadful experiences. Bobby, who is 33, experienced his first panic attack in 1987 while walking to school to take an A-level exam.

I felt very panicky and nervous, and was actually sick, which was very upsetting. I learned to associate panic with sickness. From then on it just seemed to get worse. Before doing a presentation at work I'd feel nervous and would physically be sick. I once went with some friends to a pub for lunch and started panicking about being in the car with them, fearful that I would panic and throw up.

The greatest discovery of my generation is that human beings can alter their lives by altering their state of mind.

William James

Over the next 15 years, as Bobby's life filled up with new challenges, his panic responses increased in intensity and number. 'Getting on planes, going to meetings – I was always sick before the first new experience, and from then on whenever I had to go through that experience again I lived with the fear that I might be violently unwell.'

Bobby's life was constrained by his panic responses. On the way to a meeting with his boss, he even engineered the situation so that he could take the train alone, rather than travelling by car with his colleague. But for some reason he expected his panic attacks to diminish with age. They didn't, and inevitably they began to affect his relationship with his wife. When his daughter was born, he decided it was time to seek help.

The first thing I noticed when I met Bobby was that his breathing was very shallow. When you are panicking your breath is being expelled in short sharp breaths. The focus is all on air being pushed away, so that you feel as if you have to struggle to inhale enough air to counter these rapid exhalations. It can feel like a massive undertaking just to keep enough air in your system. So, at the first sign of a panic attack, you need to change the pattern of your breathing.

You need to focus on bringing your breath back in towards you. Try it now. Take a long, slow, deep breath through your mouth, filling up your lungs completely. Don't strain to breathe, just let the air inflate your chest and fill your stomach as if you were a balloon. Then close your mouth and let the air slowly filter out through your nose.

Try the exercise on page 172, lying on your back with a book on your stomach. Breathe deeply, letting the book slowly rise and fall.

In Bobby's case, I explained to him that what was happening to him was all created by his mind. You actually have great control over your mind. You can do whatever you want with it. The resources you need are all inside yourself. Finding stillness in your mind is the first way forward. Visualization and relaxation techniques are very powerful antidotes to panic attacks.

If your heart starts to beat very quickly under the influence of too much adrenaline caused by a panic attack, one of the best things you can do is move away and do something different. Whatever you are doing, leave the room. Go outside, go to the bathroom, go for a walk, find some way of changing your state.

You can't expect to become chilled and super-relaxed overnight. But after committing himself to taking control of his thoughts, Bobby has now mastered his feelings, and you can do the same.

The real benchmark for me was going on a plane twice this year. On both occasions I had no problems at all. I even went on a fairground ride, which I'm really scared about. I told the operator I was frightened, and his response was to make the ride go even faster. I mastered my feelings and tried to enjoy it rather than freak out. I haven't had a panic attack or felt sick in months.

Of course, just *reading* about how to control your reactions isn't enough to make a change. Unless you start using these controlling techniques on a daily basis, they can't help you. 'You've got to be disciplined and remember the techniques every day,' says Bobby. 'You've also got to be determined to beat your fear.'

Helping Your Children Feel Less Afraid

Children absorb most of what they know from the world around them. Nowadays, our 'culture of caution' often stops children from playing traditional games like tag, doing handstands or even making daisy chains. A recent survey of youngsters found they were often banned from playing popular games because of adults' fears for their safety. In one case, a primary school stopped children from making daisy chains because of concerns they could pick up germs from the flowers. And at another primary school, pupils were banned from doing handstands after a girl was injured. One mother was concerned when her toddler was picked up by his arms and gently swung – she was frightened his arms were going to pop out of their sockets.

Failure to play stifles children's mental and physical development and sense of fun.

When we quiet the mind, the symphony begins.

Albert Bandura

If you really want to help your children, you won't stop them playing. Instead, you'll encourage them to discover and develop the most important thing in life: their self-esteem. But in order to do this, you first need to find your own. If you can help yourself in this way, you will help your children without even trying.

Your children are constantly watching and learning from you, but sometimes they just don't know what to do with what they are picking up. Without you even realizing it, they look to you for guidance constantly, and they are hugely sensitive.

For a GMTV special called *House of Fear* we took four seriously phobic people and helped them to conquer their fears within five days. One participant was Gillian, who, as mentioned earlier, suffered severe panic attacks when she was in confined spaces. Lifts were a nightmare for her. However, over an intensive two days she was able to work to leave her fears in the past. She is now supremely confident and is training to be a counsellor herself.

However, one thing that she learned over the course of her treatment really surprised her:

I hid my fears very well from the children, avoiding lifts altogether. The last thing I wanted was for my children to see me in this state. After I was 'cured', one day I was in a shopping centre with my children and went to take a lift, feeling full of confidence. I can still picture my five-year-old son's face. I can cry just thinking about it. Terrified, he started pulling away from me. Having recognized that look of fear on his face, there was no way I was going to force him to get into the lift. It was clear to me then that, without my even realizing it, he had completely absorbed my old fear. I'd never shown him I was frightened of lifts. I'd always go up the escalator

without mentioning a word to the children. I hadn't realized that he even knew lifts existed.

Over the course of the next few weeks Gillian used a lot of the techniques I had shown her on her son Adam.

I made it fun. I started introducing the idea of lifts as a conversational topic. We spoke about fast lifts and slow lifts, big ones and small ones. One day I told him that there was a talking lift in one shop and a completely clear glass one somewhere else. Eventually curiosity got the better of him. When we stepped inside the talking lift, I tried to give him something else to focus on. I made a game out of how long we thought it would take to go from one floor to the next. I started counting out loud in a silly voice. I said 'you were the closest there', which was a way of praising him in a roundabout way for getting in the lift and mastering his emotions.

The next time we were out shopping, he actually asked to go in the lift!

Children are amazingly adaptive. They may inherit your fear with surprising precision, but with a bit of insight and support on your part they are also able to shed unproductive behaviours quite easily. If you have a fearful child, I wholeheartedly recommend working with them in a supportive way using the ideas in this book. You will be amazed at the results.

Circumstances may cause interruptions and delay, but never lose sight of your goal. Prepare yourself in every way you can by increasing your knowledge and adding to your experience, so that you can make the most of opportunity when it occurs.

Mario Andretti

These techniques have the power to make a profound difference to your life, if you are prepared to put in the leg work. Gillian was scared of confined spaces. Of her own recovery from fear she says:

Pete encouraged me to play my fears backwards, to add imaginary music and to make my worries exaggerated in a very silly way. It was a very emotional process and quite draining, but soon I found it difficult to remember how bad I had felt, and I couldn't understand why I'd spent so many years locked into such negative programming.

I have been almost religious about using visualization and breathing exercises. I say to myself 'breathe'. It's true that, in the past, half the time I was holding my breath. It's amazing how helpful it is to focus on something else, like breathing or colour. For me, getting shot of the bad parts and replacing them with more positive thoughts felt like a form of self-hypnosis.

Soon I was looking for ways to challenge myself. The first time I got into a lift on my own was amazing. I used to concentrate on getting into a metal box encased in bricks; I was entirely focused on the negative. I will never forget the day I got into a lift by myself. I took a deep breath and said to myself, 'I'm not frightened of you.' I knew I could rise above it. The lift was orange and I had Billy Connolly in there with me. I told myself that if anything went wrong, a hunky firefighter would come and cut me out, so what did I have to lose? When the lift moved up a floor and I got out, I wanted to punch the air. That was the start of going into lifts by myself. Since then, I've been back to places that have frightened me and have been actively looking for things that will help me show myself how far I've risen above my fear.

I used to be so hyper-critical of myself, but now I help myself move forward by encouraging myself, telling myself that it's not dangerous. I now believe in myself and build myself back up if I get knocked down – these are principles that I've extended into other areas of my life. I've been down a lead mine and into caves. I've been scuba-diving. Last week I was locked in a bathroom and I didn't panic. I just knocked on the door until someone heard me. I'm a much more confident person now.

If you're comfortable where you are, fine. I'm not trying to encourage you to bungee jump or start keeping spiders as pets. If you're really happy, why change? But if you're not, you may want to start doing things differently and take on some more challenges, just as Gillian did. In fact, Gillian has gone from strength to strength. Recently she challenged herself further by going down a mineshaft where rescue teams learn their skills. She went into a number of extremely small, confined spaces, deep underground, and told me how excited and exhilarated she'd felt. Yet when we met, earlier in the year, she had dissolved in tears at the thought of climbing a poorly lit staircase by herself.

Life is not the way it's supposed to be, it's the way it is. The way you cope with it is what makes the difference.

Virginia Satir

Your 10-step Daily Fear-busting Routine

1. **The joy of each day.** The most important thing is to see every day as a blank page. See how much joy and happiness you can get out of each day, putting yesterday behind you and knowing that the future is now.

2. **Breathe deeply.** As you know from reading this book, changing the way you breathe is a pre-requisite. So start the day as you mean to go on, by practising for 4 or 5 minutes taking in lots of oxygen, filling up your stomach with air, allowing yourself to focus on yourself. Your challenge throughout the day is to see how many long, deep, nourishing breaths you can take, as they will keep you calm and relaxed.

3. **Exercise.** One of the best ways to start the day and to get your blood flowing is to do some form of exercise. This has the power to counteract the build-up of any fear chemicals, replacing them with the natural high of endorphins and serotonin, the body's natural feel-good drugs that are produced with exercise. A few sit-ups, stretches, push-ups or even a short walk outside can work wonders.

4. **Be kind to yourself.** Make contact with your inner coach and ask him or her to help you with any of the stresses and strains that might be thrown your way during the day.

5. **Forgive yourself.** Take a moment to apologize to yourself for not respecting yourself the way you should. We can all give ourselves a hard time by working too hard, being mercilessly self-critical and judging, denying ourselves enough sleep and enough of the right sort of food. Next time you are in a situation that makes you uncomfortable, try to respect your own needs. If people have a problem with you doing what you need to do, ignore them. That's their problem, not yours.

6. **Stop the water flowing out of your bath.** If you are the sort of person who is happier to give than to receive, preferring to put someone else's needs before your own or

more comfortable helping someone else rather than yourself, you are letting all the water flow out of your bath. Make a priority to keep yourself topped up by doing something for yourself each day that makes you feel good.

7. **Be responsible for how you feel.** Your challenge is to see how well you can manage your state during the day. If you start to feel stressed or anxious, fearful or worried, see how quickly you can turn your state around by focusing on something else.

8. **Eat good, wholesome and nutritious food.** You are what you eat, so it's important that you eat food that is like you: alive. Eat as much fresh, natural produce as you can – fruits, vegetables, fish, nuts, pulses, lean meat. It's not just coincidence that people who feel afraid feel hungry. Metabolized food is energizing, calming and refreshing. It's hard to be afraid when you are eating, and it's particularly difficult to stay fearful when the nutrients from the food you are eating hit your bloodstream. If you take control and make yourself eat something healthy, you'll also be less likely to snack on unhealthy foods. Keep orange juice, crisp breads, carrots, celery, apples and other healthy snacks on hand and graze on them whenever you feel peckish.

9. **Think positively.** If you're worried about the future, and about things over which you have little control, focus on all the good things in your life, perhaps even some of the things that you take for granted that enrich you. Make a list of the things in your life that you are grateful for: a wonderful family, a lovely cat, caring friends, interesting work, your health …

10. **Get plenty of sleep.** It is very difficult to feel secure and content when you are exhausted. Lack of sufficient sleep is the key trigger for fear. Reward yourself with early nights, focusing on the nourishing experience that sleep will provide. If you are unable to sleep because you are worried, don't lie in bed worrying. You will learn to associate your bed with wakefulness. Get up, walk around, drink a glass of warm milk and make a list of things that are worrying you and what you can do about them in the morning. Sit up, read a book and only go back to bed when you feel drowsy. It can also be helpful to keep a pad and pen by your bedside so you can jot down things in the night, rather than have them chasing their tails inside your head all night long.

Although you can train your body physically by sheer persistence, it's much harder to train your mind. All the visualization did not come to me in a flash. I had to work at it, and learn how to use it ... Negative thoughts lead to negative performance; the connection is as straightforward as that. The solution is to focus ... This means firstly to keep the concentration as unbroken as possible, and secondly to try to change any negative thoughts into positive ones.

Sally Gunnell

10

Turning Fear into Power

The tragedy of life is not that it ends so soon, but that we wait so long to begin it.

Like a rabbit confronted by a snake or an animal caught in car headlights, it is possible to be immobilized by fear. This is the response that bullies and muggers seek in their victims. But once you have an understanding of fear, and are familiar with the sensations that accompany it, you are in a much better position to use that rush of adrenaline to your advantage.

It is when we lose control of this energy that we descend into panic, because we don't understand what is going on in our body. But learning to harness your fear can pay enormous dividends. Fear is in fact a very positive thing, and will stand you in good stead as long as you can deploy it in your best interests, rather than allowing it to control you.

The next step in conquering your fears is actually to fall in love with them. Sounds crazy? Not really. Falling in love with fear simply means recognizing fear and using these feelings positively in your life.

Rachel Booth, a 26-year-old nurse, is constantly on call as a team member of the Northumberland National Park Search and Rescue Team. She says: 'It can be pretty tough after a long night on the wards to be woken up and called to find a lost walker, but the excitement and adrenaline keep me going.'

Sarah Parker is a lifeguard in her thirties. She says: 'The adrenaline rush and responsibility I feel when I know that a person's life depends on my actions can be intense.'

Conquering your fear does not mean destroying it. No one can ever completely destroy fear; it will always remain a vital part of your defence mechanism whether you like it or not. Instead, when you conquer something you take control of it and become its master.

Just before the 1992 Olympics 400-metres hurdle race, Sally Gunnell was feeling very scared. A gate on the other side of the stadium was open and she thought for a moment that if she ran through the gate she could escape and wouldn't have to face her fear. But instead of bolting, she used her fear in a very powerful way. By embracing her fear, within a few minutes she had turned it around and completed the race in record time.

If you face your fear with a belief, deep down, that you can overcome it, you create a situation in which you actually can.

As we saw earlier, when you focus on having done or achieved something that you fear, your brain begins to believe in the successful picture you create and doesn't realize you've made it up.

David Belle is a 28-year-old acrobat-cum-athlete who was the star of a BBC1 promotional film in spring 2002. He is the creator of a form of urban martial art called Le Parkour, whose practitioners perform daring leaps, climbs and dives across city rooftops. This real-life Spiderman performs without ropes or harnesses. The film was captivating because it was clear that what he was choosing to do was extremely dangerous. He was shown leaping 23 feet between the rooftops of two buildings more than 60 feet in the air, and landing with a perfect forward roll. In another hair-raising clip, he performed a handstand on a balustrade 120 feet above the traffic. In a manoeuvre called 'the spider' he climbed backwards up a sheer wall by bracing himself between buttresses.

Belle invented the art of Le Parkour while he was growing up in a Paris suburb in the 1980s. He inherited his love of acrobatics from his father, a circus performer in Vietnam in the 1960s.

'Parkour is a sport and an art, using all the body's muscles,' he explains. 'It is influenced by a range of heroes, including Spiderman and Bruce Lee, but also animals like the monkey, the panther and the cat. The philosophy is simple: If there is an obstacle in your way, you must find a way round it using your body and your mind.

'I was always totally obsessed with conquering my fear. I found that the more I jumped, the less afraid I became. What I do now is as much a feat of mental strength as of physical power.

'The fear is there all the time, but I am prepared. Parkour is a battle between confidence and fear – and at the moment my confidence is stronger. But you don't just go there and do it, you have to be prepared. When you are there, at the top of a tall building, you are all alone. You have to be sure of everything you do. It is dangerous, but only if you don't go at your own pace. Part of the sport's philosophy is that everyone knows their own level and

rhythm. It is like skiing, you only go on a black run if you are ready, and you make that choice yourself.'

Tom Ewart, from advertising agency Abbott Mead Vickers, which made the film for the BBC, said that it was amazing watching David in action. 'He was very calm and very focused. He would look quietly at the jump he had to make and then just go.'

We don't all want to leap off tall buildings, but the point is that fear can be your ally In everyday life as well. As Mark Twain once said: 'Courage is resistance to and mastery of fear, not the absence of fear.' My cat looks out for the dog, but he doesn't let it rule his life. If you can dare to take a risk, even when you feel frightened, the universe is likely to return your investment in your self-belief ten times over.

Learning to Take Risks

For a long time it seemed to me that life was about to begin – real life. But there was always some obstacle in the way, something to be gotten through first, some unfinished business, time still to be served, a debt to be paid. Then life would begin. At last it dawned on me that these obstacles were my life

Alfred D. Souza

Fear and excitement are closely linked because adrenaline is the root of both. One person stands on a cliff and prepares to jump 20 feet into the water below with a sense of exhilaration. Another person stands next to them and is terrified of the jump they are about to make. In both cases, external conditions are the same. The cliff is still 20 feet high; the water still seems a long way below. The difference lies in one thing alone: each person's internal expectations for the experience.

If you fear something, is it always better to walk away? Consider the jump. The person who was terrified but jumps anyway achieves mastery over their fear and immediately discovers that taking calculated risks can lead to great pay-offs. Adrenaline courses through their body and, instead of feeling nervous, they feel high, energized, amazed that they confronted their fear and proud that they did. They put themselves in control of their fearful reactions and came out on top. Next time they are faced with a similar challenge and experience those pumping feelings of anxiety, they are much more likely to make a positive association between the churning feeling of anticipation and the high this will deliver on completion of the task or challenge.

The positive benefits of facing up to your fear can apply in all areas of your life, not just the apparently adrenaline-fuelled ones. Take a look at the case of Nate, a man with a great job who decided to quit because, although impressive and well paid, it wasn't nourishing him creatively. He had no job lined up, but was armed with a feeling that he had to make a move and change his life significantly.

I'm doing it today. I have talked with a friend about it already, partly as a means to ensure that I actually DO it today ... in about 20 minutes. I've written and signed my letter of resignation. I am so nervous and anxious and excited and feel very sick.

Notice his language. He feels excited and nervous all at the same time. That's fine. His responses are due to the effects of adrenaline, and they give him this heightened emotional state. He's anxious but he's also excited.

I know what I want. I want a new sense of purpose. Just before I go in to see my boss I've got sweaty palms, an increase in my heart rate, constriction in my throat, a dry mouth, wobbly legs and a sense of nausea and butterflies; classic adrenal responses.

Of course telling his boss he was leaving was not going to end in Nate's death, but some of the sensations he was experiencing were pretty overwhelming.

I delayed all morning, then started asking myself 'Why am I making this more difficult?' I realized that I was actually *enjoying* the feelings. I knew that if I really focused on them and reminded myself that I would come out safely, then I could probably get through without any fearful feelings, but I didn't want that. I was actually getting some solidity, power and focus from these strong emotions – they were going to be my ally.

As soon as I had enough of those feelings, I put in a call to my boss to ask if I could come and see him. I was surprised just how intense the fear was, as it had been building the longer I delayed. I had started motoring around the office trying to find something to do, but settling down to anything was impossible. I was like water slowly brought to the boil; I needed that degree of agitation and powering up.

But my dialogue to myself was still all about trying to find some way out. I realized I'd spent months considering my resignation, weeks planning it, days waiting and hours avoiding it. Now I was down to minutes. I told myself all I had to do was go into a room and say a few words. That would be stage one of no turning back.

It was also the most important because it was the moment I would release the power.

I walked into my boss' office. Two things happened. First, I felt an enormous sense of relief that I had finally managed to start the process. I knew I had enough energy to complete it. I was now very focused. The butterflies had gone. The nervous energy had evaporated. In place of this was a very solid, focused energy.

The second thing that happened was that I realized I didn't know what was going to happen next. I knew what I was going to say, but I couldn't control my boss's response. Because I knew I couldn't control his response, I focused on what I *could* control: what I was going to say. I felt it was going to make a lot of sense, and that any reasonable person would understand me. I had made a feature film about it in my mind. All I had to do was push 'play'. I knew the tape was going to roll. I hadn't rehearsed the speech, but I'd rehearsed the moment when I would make the speech.

Why didn't I back out? Because resigning was what I really wanted to do. I wasn't going to let a little thing like fear get in the way. The fear strengthened my resolve. My fear was rational in that I didn't know what I would do next in my life, or whether I would find something to do before the money ran out. But I did it anyway. I knew I had to be free of the past five years before I could start the rest of my life.

I have a strong belief that things will work out. I feel confident and positive about the choices I make in life. I trust my instincts and I can see through my fears to the other side. I know they are real, but I'm not scared to feel them. Fear is always going to happen. Sometimes it's right to listen to it, sometimes it's right to face up to it, sometimes it's fun to play with it. Only you can judge for you which is the right choice. Facing fear gives you an opportunity to enjoy fearful sensations. Fear touches important dimensions of yourself; it's the reality of you. I think we can get a lot closer to dealing with fear if we are not just courageous, but also honest and keen observers.

People are not defined by whether they feel fear or not. It's what they do when they feel it that makes the difference.

It's normal to be frightened. Nate was frightened, but he dared to take the risk because he wanted to change his life. Fear gave him the boost he needed, the conviction to follow his gut, not his head, even if this felt a bit scary.

I have the courage to do the things I know I must do.

Many people are unhappy with their lives. They may not enjoy their relationships or their jobs, but they don't do anything about it. This is because they believe that anything is better than nothing. This is untrue. Change – although often extremely frightening – can be very positive.

The Power of Having Nothing to Lose

I once worked with a British athletics champion. I couldn't believe how negative he was. I found myself thinking 'How did you get into a position where you were champion?' We talked about his track record and it emerged that he had performed so badly for so long that finally he'd thought to himself 'I've got nothing to lose,' just like the British judo champion I mentioned earlier. And sure enough, once he'd entered a race with this attitude, he'd won!

Often when people say they have nothing to lose they relax a bit because they've got everything to gain, and because of this they produce a result they could never have envisaged. The danger is that they then become obsessed with analysing how they won. They start pressurizing themselves to produce the same result, failing to realize that when they succeeded there was no such expectation. It was actually the *absence* of expectations that produced the successful result in the first place.

When we have this type of positive experience, where our performance feels extraordinary and somehow effffortless, it's what athletes call 'being in the zone'. Some sportspeople believe you're lucky if you get into that space just two or three times in your career. But 'the zone' isn't something you find by accident or luck; it's always there for you to access. The way to access it is to remove all expectations and get lost in the joy of what you do.

How does this relate to you and your fears? Well, my challenge to you is to see how much joy you can get out of each moment of your life. Stop focusing on what's wrong, what's missing, your worries and your stresses, and start focusing on enjoying yourself. 'In football it's not a question of falling down, it's a question of what you do when you get up,' says Tony Adams, former Arsenal and England football captain. What he means is that bad things are always going to happen, life is like a roller-coaster, it's full of ups and downs, but next time you're in a dip say to yourself 'I'm going to enjoy this, because it isn't going to last.' Life isn't always a bowl of cherries – although, sometimes, it can be. Life is rarely the way it's supposed to be; it's just the way that it is.

The ordinary moments in life are the most difficult to appreciate, but they prepare you for great moments in the future.

Staring at a beautiful sunset, watching children at play, getting lost in a book or a fascinating movie, hearing an uplifting piece of music, enjoying a hug with someone you care for, appreciating the beautiful colours of flowers, relishing the light that spills from a full moon, savouring a nice glass of wine or guzzling a glass of ice-cold water on a hot day – when you experience moments like this you are actually in the zone. All that is going on is what you are doing, and your attention is fully present.

The golfer Tiger Woods says he's only as good as he is because he forgets the crowd is there – that's why he finds it difficult to tip his cap to the crowd. Do you know how this attitude of his came about? When he was a child his father used to stand behind him and tell him how hopeless his performance was. For a while Tiger let this affect him, but eventually he just turned around and said, 'I can't hear you, there's nothing you can say anymore.' The experience taught him to fully inhabit his own space. Such self-possession is palpable, and if the other players make the mistake of focusing on him, instead of on themselves, it means he is able to take everything away from them. The second part of Tiger's secret is that he really enjoys what he does. Other players put so much pressure on themselves that they actually lose the ability to enjoy what they're doing.

Of course most of us are not faced with the challenge of a major sporting event, but the same rules apply to any activity or endeavour where you need to pull out all the stops. People in business, actors, journalists, politicians and singers often express the idea that they are 'addicted to their own adrenaline'. What they mean is that harnessing fear is a vital part of their ability. Take away the fear and their performance is lacklustre. They need the buzz, the thrilling spark of fear to shine their brightest.

Learning to manage the benefits of fear and to embrace the positive contribution fear has to make is the final step in busting your fear.

You have two choices in life. You can either allow your fears to run your life, living in the shadow of all the awful things that have happened to you in the past. Or you can choose to harness your own strength and move on, daring yourself to see through this fear to the benefits that lie beyond it. Allow yourself to 'feel the fear and do it anyway', to immediately make big changes in your life.

A friend of mine was in a bad relationship, but she stuck with it for 10 years because she was so scared of being alone. Eventually things got so bad that she was forced to confront her fear. When her partner started beating her up she decided that her fear of being alone was a fear worth facing. She ended the relationship with a rush, a sense of confidence and self-determination that she hadn't thought possible. She is now relishing being alone and loves the opportunity her newly single state gives her to live her life on her own terms. She now can't believe that she stayed in the relationship for so long. Her fears about what breaking up would mean were all in her imagination.

Another friend of mine dreamed of building a new house. She didn't have enough money or own any land, and she was only 27. But in her mind she could see the finished home. She imagined it clearly, how it would look, how it would feel – how she would feel in it – and where it would be. She was very specific in her wishes. She imagined a country plot, on a lane, near a bluebell wood. She knew that realizing her dream would be a massive undertaking, but she only allowed herself to focus on the positives, believing that if she kept a clear picture in her head of the dream, then she could take care of all the thousands of tiny details as required. Coupled with this was a commitment to doing absolutely everything possible to follow up any leads that came her way.

Even when she was turned down by countless mortgage lenders she kept going, and eventually found a lender prepared to finance the project. She was so focused on the clear picture in her head that it helped her to stay positive and think creatively when all sorts of problems to do with planning and finances came up. The reason? She says she just couldn't conceive of everything not working out. If she had allowed herself to focus on any number of rational fears and pull back from the sometimes scary reality of her dream, she would still be dreaming. Instead, five years on, she is living in that house on a lane in a small village. And the bluebell wood is just a minute's walk away.

Make Your Own Rules

This is a new and wonderful day for me; there will never be another day like this one.

Dare to be a rebel, to make up your own rules. There is only one success: To spend your life in your own way.

Repeat this affirmation aloud: 'I've spent too much of my life doing things the way that other people have told me to do them.'

Overcoming Fear

We've all heard stories of exceptional courage – the mother who turns over a car to rescue her children who are trapped underneath; the strangers who pull drivers from burning cars that are about to explode. We believe that these people are not like us.

In actual fact, these people are *exactly* like us. The only difference is that they were placed in such an extreme situation that they had a chance to feel and act upon the mental clarity and physical strength that emerge when human beings are faced with pure terror.

Rather than being paralysed by it or running away from it (the flight response), circumstances for these people were such that they engaged with it, using the chemical cocktail to galvanize them into action (the fight response).

How can people placed in such life-or-death circumstances respond in such an apparently fearless way? And how does it make them feel?

The story of Nick Parlett, below, is an inspiring account of this galvanizing of the human spirit in the face of a truly horrific situation.

The cobalt-blue Atlantic appears deceptively calm when you peer down at it from the gorse-strewn cliffs on the southwest headland of the island of Jersey. But climb down to the surface and you can fully appreciate the power and scale of the 12-foot swell. The ocean here heaves rhythmically against the flanks of vertical, pink-flecked rocks, worn smooth after eons of wave action.

Nick was fishing off a granite ledge when he heard a cry and felt a glancing blow to his left shoulder as his friend, Peter, tripped and fell past him. 'I got shunted briefly to one side and had to watch him as he fell head-first all the way down the rocks.' It was not a clean drop. Granite boulders barred the big man's passage into the ocean, and Nick watched in horror as his 61-year-old friend bounced off the rocks below, suffering serious head injuries, before landing semi-conscious and face-down in the freezing water.

Ignoring the risk to his own safety, Nick immediately jumped 25 feet into the heavy swell. The rocks were as smooth as marble, rising sheer from the ocean. There was no time for Nick to assess how he intended to drag them both out of the icy water, but he knew he had very little time before hypothermia would claim them both.

My first thought was that Peter was dead, no one could have survived that. But then, instinctively, I knew I had to do something. I couldn't have anticipated my reaction. I made one step to climb down but suddenly what felt like a jolt of electricity just surged through my system. It wasn't an intellectual thing, and it had nothing to do with training or fitness. I simply knew I had to jump. No sooner had I had the thought, I was in the water. I grabbed Peter's jacket and pulled him over. He was barely conscious. There, in the water beside him, I had a complete shift to clarity. I knew I had to keep calm, but time felt compressed. My brain was sorting information, and normal sensory information became secondary. I didn't feel cold, despite the water being cold enough to bring on hypothermia inside 15 minutes. I didn't feel wet and had no real concept that I was in water. I felt very buoyant, like I was suspended in mid-air. It might have been different if I'd just fallen in, but my adrenaline was all directed towards Peter and getting him out. I didn't feel scared, despite the seemingly impossible situation I was in.

Holding Peter with one hand, as the swell neared its peak I reached out towards the rocks with the other. For a split second I grasped the granite, only to lose my grip when the wave receded. After five more attempts to find a crevice I could feel my energy rapidly being used up. Every time a swell dragged us halfway up the rock face, it would then drag us back down into the sea. It was then that I began to panic as my energy become momentarily less focused. I tried to block out negative thoughts, and think positively. The granite was as smooth as glass. I knew I had a short window of time; once it had passed I would no longer have enough energy to get us out of the water.

The next large wave came in and swept us a few feet higher than before. I stuffed my fingers into a crack and managed to hold on as the wave receded. Somehow, I was supporting my own weight and Peter's 15 stone, holding him above the surface of the water. I flailed with my legs and managed to get a toehold. I was shouting to Peter, 'You've got to help.' I was trying to be clear and loud and firm. I didn't know if he would lose consciousness again. The swell came back to support us and I managed to find another hand-hold. We took it one step at a time. Pete was blinded by blood and his hands were damaged, so I would reach down and kick his feet into position.

Eventually, we had climbed 25 feet and were back on the fishing ledge. Shattered to see the extent of Peter's injuries, and aware I would have to leave him to find help, I pushed his tweed trilby down over his head as a bandage. I then dragged myself back up the 200-foot cliff and ran, lungs bursting for air, to look for help. At the third house I came to someone was home, and immediately rang for an ambulance. Suddenly the adrenaline evaporated and was converted into shock. I was shattered. Soon I was crying and vomiting.

Thanks to his actions, Peter survived. He went on to make a full recovery.

A man who fears suffering is already suffering from what he fears.

Michel de Montaigne

Nick says you can't predict how you will react to such a situation until you are confronted with it. But he says that when the adrenaline rush came he understood it, and this made a big difference to the way he coped with this fearful situation. For years Nick has been extreme sea kayaking around Jersey's coastline.

Taking risks like that is all about riding your fear, understanding the effect that the adrenaline has on your body. It meant that when Peter fell and it flooded my system I didn't freeze: I acted. It's all about your reaction to that split-second and how your mind copes with an intense situation.

I call it 'positive panic'. I was firing on all cylinders, pumping pure adrenaline. Without it there is no way that I would have been able physically to drag a 15-stone man up a 25-foot cliff.

Nick was rewarded for his astonishing act of bravery with a bronze medal from The Royal Humane Society, of which the Queen is patron.

His actions, and his clear analysis of those actions, can give us an insight into the way the human mind can choose to use fear for powerfully constructive ends. The story of how he risked his own life to save his friend is one of exceptional courage and fearlessness. It reveals with almost forensic precision the way the brain can cope with such a desperate situation, and provides a clue to the incredible resources that reside inside us all. Hopefully, we'll never be placed in such terrifying circumstances. But by learning to understand fear, we give ourselves the opportunity to harness it should we ever need it.

A Short Story about Courage

A little girl named Lisa was suffering from a rare and serious disease. Her only chance of recovery appeared to be a blood transfusion from her five-year-old brother, who had miraculously survived the same disease and had developed the antibodies needed to combat it. The doctor explained the situation to the little boy and asked him if he would be willing to give his blood to his sister. He hesitated for just a moment, before taking a deep breath and saying 'Yes, I will do it, if it will save Lisa.'

As the transfusion progressed he lay in a bed next to his sister and smiled as the colour returned to her cheeks. Then his own face grew pale and his smile faded. He looked at the doctor and asked, with a trembling voice, 'Will I start to die right away?' The boy had misunderstood the doctor and had thought he was going to have to give his sister *all* his blood.

This truly inspiring story of courage and generosity also demonstrates that sometimes the thought of what we have to do is worse than the reality involved.

It's important that you take the time in life to focus on the things you *want* to have happen. If you focus on what's good, what's working, what's possible, then invariably that's what you're going to get. You don't have to believe this, but you might be surprised by the results if you give it a go.

Learning to Love Yourself Better

Being free from fear doesn't mean that you won't be affected by things that happen. Things will always happen in your life that you cannot control. But if you look after yourself, nurture your own sense of space and create a strong sense of your own security, then you have the power to become much more adept at dealing with what life throws at you.

Remember, we are the way we are through our life experiences. That's not to say that all the things that happen to us are bad, but it's a fact that many of our experiences have made us feel that we are not good enough, and this makes us frightened. How many people do you know who give themselves the respect they give to other people?

Many of our fears have come about because we believe we'll only be OK if certain things happen. This is the basis of fear – worrying how we will cope if things don't happen the way we want them to.

Discovering real faith in yourself means you can leave all that fear behind. If you allow yourself the gift of feeling totally responsible for what you think and do, then you won't care what anyone else thinks.

Falling in love with yourself is all about learning to build a much better relationship with who you really are. The fact is that if you always do what you've always done, then you'll always get what you've always got. The goal is to spend your time squeezing as much juice as you can from this thing called life, not living in fear of it. Remember, the past is over, It lives on only in your head. If you need to spring-clean the less constructive parts of your behaviour, then give yourself permission to respect yourself enough to do this.

The Reality of You

1. I'd like you to think of the various important roles you play in your life. Make a list, including such roles as friend, parent, spouse, worker, son or daughter, sister or brother. Add anything else which absorbs your time and is significant in your life.

2. Look at the first role you've written down, and consider what score you would give yourself out of 10 for the way you carry out that role. Then write that number down next to the role.

3. Do the same for each of the roles you've written down, and remember to own what you are good at.

4. Look back at the list of roles above. Now, consider that these are just roles that you play. They are not really who you are. You might have looked to define yourself by these roles, but they are not YOU.

5. You are so much more than the sum of all these roles added together. To define yourself only by the roles you play is not nourishing, because ultimately you can't have control over all the other people involved in them. You can't control the choices that your kids will make in life, you can't control the emotions of your partner, or your parents' actions or decisions. The only person you can hope to have some control over is yourself.

6. Now I'd like you to give yourself a score out of 10 for yourself. Write that number down.

7. Whatever number you've written down, I'd like you to consider something. What did you come into this world as, do you think? Of course, a 10. Well, that's still there. You are still a 10, even if you don't always feel like one.

8. Now imagine a circle on the ground just in front of you. Step into this imaginary circle and feel what it is like to be a 10. The fact that in the past you haven't thought of yourself as a 10 is probably part of the reason why you have developed fears and your particular ways of thinking. But you are a 10.

Accepting that you are a 10 doesn't mean that you are declaring that you are perfect. No one is perfect. Unfortunately, one of our biggest bad habits in the Western world is giving ourselves a hard time. We are a society that is transfixed on what is wrong, what's missing, what we haven't got. And then we wonder why we get more of it.

If you believe you are only a 1, you will move through the world as a 1. Inside you will feel like a 1, even if you are trying to project to the rest of the world that you are a 10.

You need to be your own best friend. Believing that your life will be better when you have a bigger house, a faster car, a new job, can be an illusion. Sure, you may want these things, but you need to separate want from need. You need to remind yourself, every day, no matter what, that you are a 10.

Never forget that life can only be nobly inspired and rightly lived if you take it bravely and gallantly, as a splendid adventure in which you are setting out into an unknown country, to meet many a joy, to find many a comrade, to win and lose many a battle.

Annie Besant

You may already feel differently about your fear. It may not even feel like it's yours anymore. Use the exercises in the book whenever you need to. Give yourself time to change.

And if you would like more help from one of Pete's Fear-Busting Team, please contact:

Habit Busting Limited/Pete Cohen Limited
PO BOX 2837
Leamington Spa
Warwickshire CV31 1WT
Tel: 0845 602 1607 (calls charged at local rates)
Fax: 01926 778382
Website: www.petecohen.com
Email: info@petecohen.com

Take good care of yourself.

References

Susan Balfour, *Release Your Stress* (Hodder & Stoughton, 2002)

Robert Gerzon, *Finding Serenity in the Age of Anxiety* (Bantam Doubleday Dell, 1998)

Will Horton, *Positive Mind Concepts: The Pursuit of the Enlightened 'Self'* (W.Wharton & Co, 2000)

Christine Ingham, *Panic Attacks* (Thorsons, 2000)

Susan Jeffers, *Feel the Fear and Do It Anyway: How to turn your fear and indecision into confidence and action* (Arrow, 1991)

Vera Peiffer, *Positively Fearless: Breaking Free of the Fears that Hold You Back* (Thorsons, 2001)

Index